PETER MACDONALD

NORTH AMERICAN INDIANS OF ACHIEVEMENT

PETER MACDONALD
Former Chairman of the Navajo Nation

Celia Bland

Senior Consulting Editor

W. David Baird

Howard A. White Professor of History

Pepperdine University

CHELSEA HOUSE PUBLISHERS

New York   Philadelphia

FRONTISPIECE Peter MacDonald waits to be sworn in for his fourth term as chairman of the Navajo Nation.

ON THE COVER An impassioned orator, MacDonald rallies supporters during a tumultuous phase of his political career.

Chelsea House Publishers
EDITORIAL DIRECTOR   Richard Rennert
EXECUTIVE MANAGING EDITOR   Karyn Gullen Browne
COPY CHIEF   Robin James
PICTURE EDITOR   Adrian G. Allen
ART DIRECTOR   Robert Mitchell
MANUFACTURING DIRECTOR   Gerald Levine
ASSISTANT ART DIRECTOR   Joan Ferrigno

North American Indians of Achievement
SENIOR EDITOR   Marian W. Taylor
NATIVE AMERICAN SPECIALIST   Jack Miller

Staff for PETER MACDONALD
ASSISTANT EDITOR   Margaret Dornfeld
EDITORIAL ASSISTANT   Sydra Mallery
SENIOR DESIGNER   Rae Grant
PICTURE RESEARCHER   Matthew Dudley
COVER ILLUSTRATOR   Janet Hamlin

Printed and bound in Mexico.

First Printing

1   3   5   7   9   8   6   4   2

Library of Congress Cataloging-in-Publication Data

Bland, Celia.
Peter MacDonald: Former Chairman of the Navajo Nation by Celia Bland.
    p. cm.—(North American Indians of achievement)
Includes bibliographical references and index.
ISBN 0-7910-1714-1
        0-7910-2071-1 (pbk.)
1. MacDonald, Peter, 1928– —Juvenile literature. 2. Navajo Indians—Biography—Juvenile literature. 3. Navajo Indians—Kings government—Juvenile literature. 4. Navajo Indians—Politics and government—Juvenile literature. I.Title.

E99.N3M28 1995   94-21856
979.1'004972—dc20   CIP
[B]   AC

CONTENTS

NORTH AMERICAN INDIANS OF ACHIEVEMENT

Other titles in preparation

ON INDIAN LEADERSHIP

by W. David Baird
Howard A. White Professor of History
Pepperdine University

Authoritative utterance is in thy mouth, perception is in thy heart, and thy tongue is the shrine of justice," the ancient Egyptians said of their king. From him, the Egyptians expected authority, discretion, and just behavior. Homer's *Iliad* suggests that the Greeks demanded somewhat different qualities from their leaders: justice and judgment, wisdom and counsel, shrewdness and cunning, valor and action. It is not surprising that different people living at different times should seek different qualities from the individuals they looked to for guidance. By and large, a people's requirements for leadership are determined by two factors: their culture and the unique circumstances of the time and place in which they live.

Before the late 15th century, when non-Indians first journeyed to what is now North America, most Indian tribes were not ruled by a single person. Instead, there were village chiefs, clan headmen, peace chiefs, war chiefs, and a host of other types of leaders, each with his or her own specific duties. These influential people not only decided political matters but also helped shape their tribe's social, cultural, and religious life. Usually, Indian leaders held their positions because they had won the respect of their peers. Indeed, if a leader's followers at any time decided that he or she was out of step with the will of the people, they felt free to look to someone else for advice and direction.

Thus, the greatest achievers in traditional Indian communities were men and women of extraordinary talent. They were not only skilled at navigating the deadly waters of tribal politics and cultural customs but also able to, directly or indirectly, make a positive and significant difference in the daily life of their followers.

From the beginning of their interaction with Native Americans, non-Indians failed to understand these features of Indian leadership. Early European explorers and settlers merely assumed that Indians had the same relationship with their leaders as non-Indians had with their kings and queens. European monarchs generally inherited their positions and ruled large nations however they chose, often with little regard for the desires or needs of their subjects. As a result, the settlers of Jamestown saw Pocahontas as a "princess" and Pilgrims dubbed Wampanoag leader Metacom "King Philip," envisioning them in roles very different from those in which their own people placed them.

As more and more non-Indians flocked to North America, the nature of Indian leadership gradually began to change. Influential Indians no longer had to take on the often considerable burden of pleasing only their own people; they also had to develop a strategy of dealing with the non-Indian newcomers. In a rapidly changing world, new types of Indian role models with new ideas and talents continually emerged. Some were warriors; others were peacemakers. Some held political positions within their tribes; others were writers, artists, religious prophets, or athletes. Although the demands of Indian leadership altered from generation to generation, several factors that determined which Indian people became prominent in the centuries after first contact remained the same.

Certain personal characteristics distinguished these Indians of achievement. They were intelligent, imaginative, practical, daring, shrewd, uncompromising, ruthless, and logical. They were constant in friendships, unrelenting in hatreds, affectionate with their relatives, and respectful to their God or gods. Of course, no single Native American leader embodied all these qualities, nor these qualities only. But it was these characteristics that allowed them to succeed.

The special skills and talents that certain Indians possessed also brought them to positions of importance. The life of Hiawatha, the legendary founder of the powerful Iroquois Confederacy, displays the value that oratorical ability had for many Indians in power.

The biography of Cochise, the 19th-century Apache chief, illustrates that leadership often required keen diplomatic skills not only in transactions among tribespeople but also in hardheaded negotiations with non-Indians. For others, such as Mohawk Joseph Brant and Navajo Peter MacDonald, a non-Indian education proved advantageous in their dealings with other peoples.

Sudden changes in circumstance were another crucial factor in determining who became influential in Indian communities. King Philip in the 1670s and Geronimo in the 1880s both came to power when their people were searching for someone to lead them into battle against white frontiersmen who had forced upon them a long series of indignities. Seeing the rising discontent of Indians of many tribes in the 1810s, Tecumseh and his brother, the Shawnee prophet Tenskwatawa, proclaimed a message of cultural revitalization that appealed to thousands. Other Indian achievers recognized cooperation with non-Indians as the most advantageous path during their lifetime. Sarah Winnemucca in the late 19th century bridged the gap of understanding between her people and their non-Indian neighbors through the publication of her autobiography *Life Among the Piutes*. Olympian Jim Thorpe in the early 20th century championed the assimilationist policies of the U.S. government and, with his own successes, demonstrated the accomplishments Indians could make in the non-Indian world. And Wilma Mankiller, principal chief of the Cherokees, continues to fight successfully for the rights of her people through the courts and through negotiation with federal officials.

Leadership among Native Americans, just as among all other peoples, can be understood only in the context of culture and history. But the centuries that Indians have had to cope with invasions of foreigners in their homelands have brought unique hardships and obstacles to the Native American individuals who most influenced and inspired others. Despite these challenges, there has never been a lack of Indian men and women equal to these tasks. With such strong leaders, it is no wonder that Native Americans remain such a vital part of this nation's cultural landscape.

1

THE MOST
POWERFUL INDIAN
IN THE UNITED STATES

He is my son, for he is my sister's son," 72-year-old Minnie Saltwater explained to the reporter from the *Navajo Times*. "I have come to see my son take office again."

Resplendent in her best turquoise and silver jewelry and her finest velveteen blouse, Mrs. Saltwater had traveled more than 100 miles to attend Peter MacDonald's inauguration. Today, at the Window Rock, Arizona, fairground, he would begin an unprecedented fourth term as Navajo tribal chairman. More than 15,000 people had turned out on this cold day in January 1987 to await the new chairman's motorcade—the first such parade in Navajo history.

"I've been sitting here since before the snow began to melt this morning," Frank Tohani told the reporter. "Delightful," he added, hitting the bleachers with his open palm and nodding with satisfaction at the be-ribboned grandstand below.

A wooden platform rising out of the fairground mud, the grandstand was lined with dignitaries. Such political

Peter MacDonald relaxes at Navajo government headquarters during his first term as tribal chairman.

figures as Arizona governor Evan Mecham, the Reverend Jesse Jackson, the secretary for Indian affairs, the U.S. energy secretary, and congressional representatives from Utah, Colorado, Arizona, and New Mexico had come to honor the chairman-elect. Behind these men billowed a huge tapestry colorfully patterned with traditional Navajo designs. This was the Chilchinbeto rug, displayed at all the tribal swearing-in ceremonies—rituals the Navajos called "holding the hand up."

Gathered together on metal bleachers, the Navajo crowd cheered wildly as the motorcade drove into sight, and MacDonald, dapper in an expertly tailored suede jacket and dark glasses, got out of a white limousine. The cheering continued as the vice chairman-elect, Johnny Thompson, appeared from a second car.

Navajo police officers stationed atop a nearby building surveyed the crowd warily, their rifles at the ready. Television reporters from the Navajo Cable Systems Network were jostled to one side as the throng clamored to see the elected men make their way to the grandstand. When his supporters began to chant, "Bring class back to government!" Peter MacDonald's heavily lined face relaxed into a delighted grin.

On reaching the grandstand, MacDonald shook hands with the visiting dignitaries, accepting their congratulations. He then approached the podium, taking his place beneath the Navajo tribal seal. As he looked out over the sea of smiling faces, his usually somber demeanor brightened and, beaming, he raised his arms above his head in a fighter's gesture of triumph.

This 58-year-old man had traveled a long road. Through years of hard work and perseverance, he had risen from a small, mud-covered hogan (the traditional Navajo dwelling) in the arid hills of Teec Nos Pos, Arizona, to the chairman's office—so luxurious it was

A triumphant chairman MacDonald waves to the crowd during his 1987 inauguration at Window Rock, Arizona, as his wife, Wanda (left), and members of the Navajo Tribal Court look on.

known as the Mahogany Palace—and the position of *naat'anii*, leader of *Diné* (the Navajo people). MacDonald's intelligence, tenacity, and capacity for hard work had led him from poverty to wealth, from obscurity to fame—but not without episodes of hardship, humiliation, and scandal along the way.

The ceremony opened with a message of congratulations from President Ronald Reagan. Then a hush fell over the assembly as incumbent chairman Peterson Zah

and his wife, Rosalyn, walked from their battered pickup truck to their seats in the bleachers. There was a burst of applause, and the Zahs were formally recognized by the platform. Many Navajos respected Zah's lack of ostentation, and on this day of MacDonald's triumphant return, Zah's modesty contrasted sharply with the new chairman's love of spectacle and pomp.

Justice Tom Tso administered the oath of office to Chairman MacDonald and Vice-Chairman Thompson, and they were blessed by a medicine man. Then MacDonald turned to address the crowd. In a voice hoarse with emotion, he said simply, "Today I feel I have completed a long and difficult journey and have returned home to serve my people."

MacDonald's journey had begun 24 years earlier, in 1963, when he was a member of the technical staff at the Hughes Aircraft Corporation and in charge of a multimillion-dollar U.S. Navy contract for the development, manufacture, and delivery of the Polaris missile guidance system. In contrast to most of the Navajos he had grown up with, MacDonald had succeeded in the non-Indian world, and to a large extent, he was living the American dream. With his wife, Ruby, MacDonald was raising his children, Peter, Jr., (nicknamed Rocky), and Linda, in a suburb of El Segundo, California.

McDonald's career took him far away from the world of his childhood, and he had to make a special effort to stay in touch with his Navajo heritage. He visited his mother on the Navajo reservation once or twice a year and helped his extended family with money and advice. But he often wished he could do more. Even on brief visits to the reservation, MacDonald could see that the Navajos were in dismal need of his hard-won expertise. Conditions on the reservation were even worse in 1963 than when MacDonald had left 15 years earlier to attend

A lone rider surveys Monument Valley, an arid region in the northeast corner of the Navajo Reservation, near Peter MacDonald's birthplace.

college. The Navajo population had swelled from 65,000 to more than 90,000, and roughly 20,000 of these people were unemployed. The only thriving businesses were the bars lining the reservation's borders.

MacDonald soon received his opportunity to help. Hoping to improve life on the reservation, in 1963 tribal chairman Raymond Nakai asked the young engineer if he would come work for the Navajo government and help reorganize the tribe's investments. Nakai believed MacDonald would be able to attract businesses to the Navajo reservation, which was rich in precious natural resources. Rising to the challenge, MacDonald obtained a year's leave of absence from the Hughes corporation and moved with his family to Fort Defiance, Arizona, near Window Rock, the seat of the tribal government.

Soon after his return to the reservation, MacDonald sat in on a Tribal Council meeting. He was observing the proceedings when Glen Landbloom, the Bureau of Indian Affairs (BIA) representative, interrupted a heated debate between two Navajo council members. Landbloom pounded on the podium impatiently, calling the men to order. "If you guys continue to act like children," MacDonald remembers him telling them, "I'm going to throw every one of you out of this council chamber. I'm going to put a padlock on it. And I'm not going to let you back in until you learn to behave like adults!"

MacDonald was shocked by Landbloom's patronizing tone. "This Landbloom guy was treating the council like it was back in 1700!" he recalled in a 1989 *New York Times Magazine* article. "I couldn't get over it. So I said to myself, 'One of these days, it's not going to be like that.'"

MacDonald set to work finding ways to improve the Navajo economy, determined that his people should benefit from the War on Poverty legislation just enacted by President Lyndon B. Johnson's administration. In 1965 he helped the tribe win a grant of $900,000 from the Economic Opportunity Act, and he was soon named executive director of the Office of Navajo Economic Opportunity (ONEO). Throwing himself into this new role, MacDonald insisted that federal monies be paid directly to the ONEO rather than to white administrators at the Bureau of Indian Affairs. After two years on the job, he had organized a $12 million antipoverty program financed by the federal government. He had also made a name for himself as an energetic administrator and shrewd negotiator.

With these successes behind him, and eager to expand his authority in the Navajo Nation, in 1970 MacDonald made a bold move: he challenged Raymond Nakai in his bid for a third term as tribal chairman. The Navajo Nation had never granted any chairman a third term, and Nakai, a former encyclopedia salesman, was outstripped by MacDonald, with his record of administrative successes and his superior speaking ability. "He had something that Nakai didn't have," Nakai's former aide told *Mother Jones* magazine in 1982. "Maybe it was charisma. . . . He'd come into council chambers and deliver fiery speeches against the white man, the BIA, the energy companies—you name it. Later he just turned it all against Nakai himself." Betty Reid, a reporter for the Gallup, New Mexico, *Independent*, agreed. "It was just amazing," she said in an interview. "People hung on his every word. He has this gift. If you listen to him speak in Navajo, it's incredible."

MacDonald won the 1970 election by a landslide, and he was re-elected in 1974 and 1978. In every campaign he stressed Navajo self-determination and self-sufficiency, even as he boasted of his close ties to the federal government. In 1978, he distributed campaign flyers picturing himself shaking hands with President Jimmy

Carter above a caption reading, "The Most Powerful and Influential Indian in the United States."

MacDonald's power, however, was not secure. In 1976, for example, he came close to losing his position when he was charged with submitting false travel vouchers to Tucson Gas & Electric Company. MacDonald had allegedly accepted kickbacks (secret payments) in exchange for helping the company win a lucrative contract to build power lines across the reservation. With the help of an expert defense lawyer, F. Lee Bailey, MacDonald was acquitted of all criminal charges in that case, but his troubles were just beginning. By the mid-1970s, a bitter political feud between MacDonald and Arizona senator Barry Goldwater had caused a rift in the chairman's influence outside the Navajo community. Partly as a result of this decline in support, in 1974 a long-standing land dispute between the Navajos and their Native American neighbors, the Hopis, culminated in a law that would force more than 6,000 Navajos to leave their farms and ranches in the land claimed by the Hopis and resettle in another part of Navajo territory. By 1980, U.S. officials had begun to implement this ruling, and a number of Navajo families had faced the emotional and spiritual hardship of relocation.

Many Navajo voters deeply resented MacDonald for allowing the removal law to go into effect, and they displayed their feelings in the next election. In 1982, after a fierce campaign, MacDonald was deposed by Peterson Zah, director of Dinébeiina Nahiilna Be Agaditahe (DNA), the Navajo legal service that MacDonald had founded during his days at the ONEO.

MacDonald returned to the business world, working as director of sales and marketing for a company called Cataract, Inc. Again he proved a shrewd negotiator, and the company made great financial gains during his tenure

Peter and Wanda MacDonald, with Navajo beauty queen Audra Arviso, celebrate the chairman's return to office at an inaugural ball in Gallup, New Mexico.

there. Meanwhile, Chairman Zah did his best to enact government reforms on the Navajo reservation. Unfortunately for Zah, however, it was at this point that the federal government, under the administration of President Ronald Reagan, began cutting back aid to the Indians. The Navajo economy suffered a severe recession, and by the time the 1986 elections came around, many people were ready to throw their support back to MacDonald, who promised that his expertise in negotiating leases with energy companies would help the Navajos weather hard times. Now the former chairman was ready to return to power.

Peter MacDonald stood alone at the podium. He had come here on this sunny January day to accept his people's challenge. Could he, in Peterson Zah's words, "be honest and live by what he says"? MacDonald boldly proclaimed that he could. "Let us forge ahead along the path toward economic self-sufficiency," he cried. "Let us, once and for all, share in the bounty of America. I am here because you believed in me." Rapidly he sketched his plans to increase the monies available for college scholarships, to streamline bureaucracy, and to smooth the way for big business to build factories on the reservation. "Our hibernation is over," he told his people. "A new spring is just beginning to dawn across this wonderful land of ours. Together we have . . . together we can . . . and together we *will* surely triumph."

MacDonald's words were greeted by sustained applause and loud cheering. Once again, he had communicated his enthusiasm to the crowd, instilling hope and confidence in his people. Not everyone was equally convinced of the chairman's sincerity, however. As the spectators slowly left the fairground, Raymond Benally, a tribe member from Church Rock, New Mexico, paused to speak with a *New York Times* reporter. "He promised a lot of things before that he never fulfilled," Benally said. "This thing about college education is just another gimmick." Cecil Largo from Window Rock agreed. "Mr. MacDonald just promised too many things he knows he can't deliver. He said the same old thing."

Those who attended the inaugural ball in Gallup, New

Mexico, may well have agreed that, at least in one respect, MacDonald had not changed. Dancing with his second wife, Wanda, to the tune of "The Tennessee Waltz," MacDonald and his friends were enjoying an opulent evening valued at $10,000. The bill for the inaugural celebration as a whole would soon be presented to a financially strapped Tribal Council. It totaled $40,000.

Navajo

Pennington

2

THE CREATION OF PETER MACDONALD

Peter MacDonald was born near the northeast corner of Arizona in the spring of 1928, while his family was driving sheep from the open range toward their home near Teec Nos Pos. According to MacDonald's autobiography, *The Last Warrior*, the family prepared for the birth in the traditional manner. His great aunt, who was traveling with his mother, "did what Navajo women had been doing for generations," he explains. "First, she found a sturdy piece of wood that would serve as a pole. Then she dug a hole deep enough so that the pole could be tightly inserted, reinforced with dirt, and made to hold fast. She tied a rope around the top of the pole so that my mother could pull down on it during the labor contractions, and she placed a goatskin pad beneath my mother so that I would have a soft resting place when I was born." MacDonald's parents called him Hoshkaisith (He Who Grabs with Strength) and raised him according to Navajo custom.

Hoshkaisith's family, the Begay clan, was wealthy, owning 5,000 sheep, 2,000 cows, and more than 300 horses. Every year the clan members traveled with their herds from their summer home in Teec Nos Pos into the Arizona mountains and on toward their grazing lands in

Peter MacDonald's maternal grandfather, Deshna Clah Cheschillige, was a leading member of the Begay clan, a well-to-do family centered in northeast Arizona.

MacDonald's mother, Lucy Ute Bileen, appears in a photograph taken in the early 1950s. Originally named Hoshkaisith Begay, Peter MacDonald was raised according to Navajo tradition near his mother's hogan in Teec Nos Pos, Arizona.

Utah, where they camped for the winter. They moved south again in the spring.

Driving their livestock over the arid southwestern lands in this way, the Begays were carrying on a Navajo tradition that had existed for more than 700 years. Like all Navajos, the Begays were descendants of a fierce group of wanderers who appeared in the Southwest around 1300 A.D. Calling themselves *diné,* or "the people," the first

Navajos migrated to the rocky canyons and desert plateaus of New Mexico and Arizona from the cold shores of Lake Athabasca in Canada's Northwest Territory. The Navajos adapted quickly to their new environment, appropriating fresh skills from neighboring tribes. They learned sheep-herding, farming, basketry, and pottery from the Pueblos, and they mastered the Hopi arts of silversmithing and weaving so thoroughly that Navajo jewelry and blankets are now sought by collectors around the world.

Despite these changes, the Navajos retained firm ties to their nomadic past. They never developed large, permanent villages such as those of the Pueblo Indians. Instead, Navajo clans, or extended families, lived together in temporary encampments, herding livestock over wide stretches of isolated landscape. The Navajos grew deeply attached to their home in the Southwest; most of their clan names refer to the Indians' herding routes or encampment sites, and their religion drew inspiration from the four sacred mountains that mark the boundaries of their reservation.

From the moment he was born, Hoshkaisith Begay, like other Navajo children, was almost always on the move. When he was two years old, his father was killed in a riding accident, and the boy grew up under the firm hand of his grandfather, a powerful medicine man. While he was still a young boy Hoshkaisith experienced yet another serious loss. He and his younger sister, Betty, were napping by the fire at the family's winter campsite while their older relatives rounded up the horses and sheep. Suddenly Betty let out a high-pitched scream. Her clothes had been set alight by the fire's embers, and by the time Hoshkaisith had put out the flames by wrapping her in a blanket, she had been terribly burned. She died a few days later. Hoshkaisith never forgave himself for falling asleep and allowing the accident to happen. His

mother mourned the little girl for many years, repeatedly telling her son of the prophetic dream she had dreamed the night before the accident, in which an owl called Betty's name.

As Hoshkaisith grew older, he began working at his grandfather's side, absorbing the fine points of animal husbandry and farming. Soon he was helping out by herding hundreds of spring lambs through the red clay washes and desert pastures of the Navajo reservation, a 25,000-square-mile area spread over northeast Arizona, northwest New Mexico, and southeast Utah. Every spring the boy watched as his mother, grandmother, and sisters sheared the sheep, holding the animals firmly and cutting the wool with sharp knives. The wool was then carded and spun into coarse thread and used to weave beautifully patterned blankets. Some of these blankets were so closely woven they were water-resistant. Every part of the sheep was used by the family: its wool became clothing or bedding, its meat and brains were eaten, and its hide was tanned for moccasins.

Some 15 adults, all members of the Begay clan, lived together in the winter and summer camps, helping each other tend the herds and cultivate squash, corn, wheat, and fruit. Married couples and their children lived together in their own hogans, prepared their own food, and tended their own horses, but the large herds of livestock were considered community property, and the adults and children of the clan all took part in caring for them and enjoyed a share of their milk, wool, and meat. The young cousins worked and played together and formed close bonds of loyalty and competition. Strict rules, however, forbade romances between girls and boys of the same clan. Navajo tradition has always prohibited intermarriage within a clan, and even today a relationship of this kind brings terrible shame upon the family.

A Navajo weaver creates a boldly patterned rug, practicing a craft her people learned from the Hopis hundreds of years earlier. Prized for their beauty and durability, Navajo rugs remain one of the tribe's main sources of income.

Unlike many other tribes, the Navajos did not have a central government or a principal leader in the early 1930s, when Hoshkaisith was growing up. They lived in small, isolated, self-sufficient communities, tending their herds and fields, and their contact with other clans was limited to religious festivals and clan celebrations. Hoshkaisith's maternal grandparents headed his family, and his parents, uncles, aunts, and cousins lived by the grandparents' decisions. Within the clan as a whole, the older man deemed wisest generally served as the group's spokesman and spiritual leader.

It was not until the late 1930s that the Navajos followed the lead of the Utes, Hopis, and other south-western Indians in creating the position of tribal chair-

Members of a Navajo family gather outside their hogan at Grey Mountain, near the southern rim of the Grand Canyon. In most ways the life of the Begays, a prosperous clan, resembled that of less fortunate Navajos, for to live according to Navajo tradition meant to live simply.

man. The Indians developed this position hoping to gain more control over their relations with U.S. officials, who sought the use of their lands and insisted on negotiating with them through an individual leader. The Navajos and other tribes had found that if they did not elect their own spokesperson, officials would simply appoint a "false chief" who would agree to unfair treaties or land leases affecting the entire tribe.

By the 1930s, the Indians' dealings with the government had already brought them many hardships, including an ordeal known as the Long Walk, the most painfully remembered event in Navajo history. Relations between the Navajos and the non-Indians who lived near them had been tense for more than a hundred years.

Ever since they first settled in the Southwest, Navajo warriors had engaged in raids against the Hopis, Utes, and Apaches, robbing them of livestock and taking prisoners whom they kept as slaves. Starting in the 1600s, when Spanish colonists began moving into their region, the Navajos attacked European settlements as well, and their assaults became more frequent as the white population grew. By the early 19th century, hostilities between the Navajos and their non-Indian neighbors had escalated dramatically. New Mexico settlers eventually went so far as to hire vigilantes to raid Navajo encampments and take prisoners to be employed as slaves. These operations were very successful; it is estimated that as late as 1860, the New Mexicans held more than 5,000 Navajo slaves.

Finally the U.S. government intervened, sending agents to the Navajo camps to negotiate for an end to the fighting. The officials were able to make treaties with some of Navajo clans, but not with all, and many of the Indians who had not signed the treaties refused to honor them. The violence continued. In 1851, the U.S. War Department built Fort Defiance in central New Mexico Territory to monitor and contain the Navajo assaults, but

Colonel Kit Carson
of the First New Mexico
Volunteers led a massive
campaign against the Navajos
in 1863. As a result of his
efforts, some 8,000 members
of the tribe surrendered
to government agents and
were forced to walk more
than 250 miles to a small,
barren reservation in
eastern New Mexico.

for many years the Indians continued to outwit and outfight the U.S. cavalry. In 1862, the government renewed its efforts and built Fort Wingate some 100 miles southeast of Fort Defiance.

In 1863, Kit Carson, a renowned trapper and explorer and a colonel of the First New Mexico Volunteers, set out to subdue the Navajos once and for all. Traveling from camp to camp, Carson's men systematically seized the

Indians' livestock and destroyed their crops, killing those who tried to resist. Thousands of Navajos escaped and fled into the mountains, but the harsh winter and the Indians' hunger forced most of them to leave their hiding places and surrender to the authorities at Forts Defiance and Wingate.

In 1864, the 8,000 Navajos camped at these forts were forced to walk more than 250 miles to Bosque Redondo, a reservation the government had established near Fort Sumner in the eastern part of the New Mexico Territory. The Long Walk, as the journey came to be known, was a brutalizing experience. According to Peter MacDonald, those who went through it "never forgot the horrors they witnessed and endured." MacDonald's great-grandmother, a Long Walk survivor, later told stories of the babies she had seen being carried along the trail, their tiny bellies swollen with starvation, their mouths screaming at their mothers' shriveled breasts. MacDonald would always remember her warning: "It could happen again."

As a child, Hoshkaisith Begay participated in a ritual the Navajos had developed as a way of commemorating the Long Walk. Every morning, just as the sun peeked over the horizon, he and the other children in his camp were roused by their parents and brought outside to face the east. They were given a small bag of corn pollen to sprinkle into the air, and with their faces upturned to the sun, they ran as fast as they could for a mile or more.

"All the children ran," MacDonald remembered, "no matter what their age. Uncles and grandfathers would run, too, to keep fit themselves and to make certain everyone completed the required mile or two." These morning runs were designed to prepare the youths for an enemy attack; during the violent raids that preceded the Long Walk, fast running had sometimes made the difference between freedom and captivity.

After the Long Walk, the Navajos at Bosque Redondo had been instructed to set up farms to support themselves, but the few crops they were able to grow were destroyed by flood, drought, hail, and insects. Much of their livestock fell to the Comanches, a nearby tribe who made frequent raids on the reservation. The rations the government offered the Navajos barely kept them alive. For four years the Indians lived in utter destitution, many of them dying of malnutrition, exposure, and disease. Then, in 1868, the U.S. government suggested that the tribe move to a reservation in Oklahoma. A celebrated Navajo warrior named Barboncito, acting as spokesman for his people, proposed that the Navajos instead be allowed to return to their old homelands, telling U.S. authorities, "After we get back to our country it will brighten up again and the Navajos will be as happy as the land." Eventually, the government acquiesced, and the Navajos were given 3.5 million acres in what is now northeastern Arizona and northwestern New Mexico. The Navajos agreed that railroad companies could lay tracks across their lands with impunity; they were to be issued farming equipment and livestock, and their children were to be sent to government-sponsored schools.

It was at one of these institutions—a boarding school run by the Bureau of Indian Affairs at Teec Nos Pos—that six-year-old Hoshkaisith Begay received the name he is known by today. The boy had been sent by his mother to draw water from the school's well when he was noticed by a teacher and invited inside. Hoshkaisith was immediately given a bath, clean clothes, hard-soled shoes, and a haircut. When his worried mother came looking for him, the teacher convinced her that Hoshkaisith should stay at the school and learn to add, subtract, and read and write the English language.

Hoshkaisith had already been christened Peter by a

local trader, and his mother offered this name when she enrolled him at the school. When asked for the name of the boy's father, she refused to answer, for it is a Navajo custom never to speak of the dead. A mispronunciation of his grandfather's name eventually produced the surname "Donald," and Hoshkaisith Begay began his formal education as Peter Donald. Some time later, when his classmates learned the song "Old MacDonald," they playfully switched to calling him Peter MacDonald, and the name held.

As a boarder at the BIA school, Peter enjoyed his lessons—particularly mathematics—but felt angry and humiliated when his teachers ridiculed Navajo customs. The school administrators maintained that Indian ways were inferior to those of whites and that Native Americans should dress like white people, live in houses rather than hogans, and, as one poster distributed by missionaries dictated, "believe that property and wealth are signs of divine approval." The traditional Navajo diet of mutton stew, fried bread, and blue cornmeal mush was considered less nutritious than the white people's steak and french fries. Navajo children were even punished for speaking their own language.

At the age of 12, Peter ran away from school and returned to his family. Soon he was acting as his grandfather's apprentice, learning the Navajo religious rituals called the chantways. Only after 5 to 10 years of arduous spiritual training would he be qualified to act as medicine man, the keeper of the ancient traditions.

But to his grandfather's disappointment, Peter did not complete his religious education. At 14, he decided instead to seek paid work so that he could better help his family. The once prosperous Begays were now impoverished, for they had lost hundreds of cattle and sheep in a government livestock-reduction program. In the 1930s and

1940s, government analysts had decided that the Navajos' herds of cattle and sheep were contributing to the erosion of the desert soil. Silt from the lands their animals grazed was being carried into the rivers and clogging the recently built Boulder Dam (later renamed the Hoover Dam). Hoping to stop this process, the U.S. government had forced the Navajos to reduce their herds. Now, like so many other Navajos, Peter's mother was wearing rags, and the boy's shoes were little more than strips of leather.

In 1942, Peter went to work shoveling wood pulp at a lumberyard in Colorado. With his first paycheck he bought a pair of jeans and some new boots; the rest of the money was sent home to his mother. Peter did not stay at the lumberyard for very long. The attitude of the white foreman there—he yelled, "Dirty Indian, lazy Indian," whenever Peter made a mistake—soon prompted the boy to apply for a better-paying job with the Union Pacific Railroad. Unfortunately, he had to convince the Union Pacific foreman that he was 17, the legal age for employment. Peter's cousin suggested that he go to the local draft board, tell them he was 17, register for the draft, and get a draft card to show the foreman as proof of his age. Peter followed his cousin's advice and was soon working with a Union Pacific crew laying rails in Oregon. A short time later he received a notice from the U.S. government; he had been drafted into active service in World War II.

MacDonald's paternal grandfather, a medicine man, played an important role in his upbringing. Known as Dahgahlani, or "Many Whiskers," he taught Peter how to perform the Navajo healing rituals known as the chantways.

In 1944, at the age of 15, Peter MacDonald became a U.S. marine. He eventually joined the code talkers, a select group of Navajos who transmitted military communications over the radio in a code based on their own language. For two years he helped establish communication posts, first at Pearl Harbor, Hawaii, and then in China.

One night when MacDonald was still at boot camp, a

At the age of 15, Peter MacDonald became a U.S. marine. He soon joined the code talkers, a communications unit that transmitted messages in a code based on the Navajo language.

private came to him with a letter he had received and asked the young Navajo to read the letter aloud. MacDonald warily complied, afraid that the soldier was playing a trick on the "dumb Indian." But the next day, when the young man returned and asked him to write a letter in response, MacDonald understood why the private had approached him: the boy could neither read nor write, and he was asking MacDonald to help him.

This seemingly minor incident left a deep impression on MacDonald. "I always thought, up to that point," he told a *New York Times* reporter in 1971, "that white men were born already knowing how to write and read. It really changed my attitude. I decided, hey, these guys don't have any secret endowment, as they say they do. They're not any better than I am. . . . From that day on, I never bowed down to anybody."

In *The Last Warrior*, MacDonald wrote, "The BIA schools had drilled one consistent thought into my mind—that I was inferior to others. I was poor, dirty, and ignorant. . . . Once I realized that white people didn't have any more skills than I did unless they got an education, I no longer thought of them as a super race." Having realized that everything non-Indians valued lay within his grasp, MacDonald decided he would do his utmost to become educated in the ways of the white world. He would compete against whites—and win.

3

▼ ▼ ▼

"BORN A NAVAJO!"

A veteran at the age of 17, Peter MacDonald returned
home in 1946 to find that wartime prosperity had not
reached the Navajo reservation; his people were living in
even greater poverty than before. Unemployment was
widespread, and many of MacDonald's fellow veterans,
unable to find work, turned to alcohol as a way of
numbing their frustration.

MacDonald worked briefly for the U.S. Parks Service
in Navajo country, performing traditional dances for
tourists, then decided he would go back to school and
learn a skill, hoping eventually to get a good job that
would help him support his family. He enrolled at a trade
school in Fort Wingate, New Mexico, and within two
semesters he had passed a high school equivalency test.

MacDonald's teachers encouraged him to continue his
studies, and in 1949 he entered Bacone College, a Baptist
institution in Oklahoma. To his dismay, an intelligence
test at Bacone scored him at "moron" level, and the school
required him to retake examinations he had already
passed with honors. Yet MacDonald had happy experi-
ences at Bacone as well: it was there that he met and
married his first wife, Ruby Wallace, a member of the
Comanche tribe.

After two years at Bacone, MacDonald transferred to the University of Oklahoma in Norman. There, still troubled by the "moron" rating, he declared a major in electrical engineering, the field he was told was the hardest to master. MacDonald had come a long way from shoveling wood pulp, but he still had a difficult road to travel. He took classes during the day, minded his baby son, Peter, Jr., in the afternoon, and worked nights at the Norman mental hospital. Finally, in 1957, he graduated from the University of Oklahoma with a bachelor of science degree, and he was immediately offered a $5,000-a-year position as junior engineer at Hughes Aircraft. MacDonald admired the company's founder, the multimillionaire Howard Hughes, and he took the job. As soon as he started, MacDonald set to work to prove himself;

Millionaire Howard Hughes takes a short break between meetings in the backseat of his car. After graduating from college, MacDonald worked at Hughes Aircraft Corporation, a company founded by the celebrated businessman.

the Hughes corporation, he later commented, did not "put me in a position. . . . They expected me to earn a position." MacDonald worked long nights and was rewarded with a promotion to senior engineer in just 18 months. In six years he was a member of the company's technical staff and the director of a multimillion-dollar contract with the navy for the development, manufacture, and delivery of the Polaris missile guidance system. MacDonald commanded a salary of $18,000 a year, and he was moving toward the upper echelons of the engineering industry. Yet he found that he missed the hands-on work of planning and supervising engineering projects. Life on Mahogany Row, as he nicknamed the corporate offices at Hughes, was less challenging than the nuts and bolts of planning individual projects and seeing them through to completion.

In 1963, MacDonald was offered an alternative to his business career. As he explained in *The Last Warrior,* "I learned that Raymond Nakai [a distant cousin] had been elected Navajo tribal chairman. . . . He wanted to see if the decline into poverty and despair could be reversed. To do this, he was seeking Navajo men and women with skills not normally associated with the tribe. One of the people whose name had arisen during this search was mine." Flattered, MacDonald agreed to take a leave of absence from his job at Hughes in order to play a role in the Navajo tribal government. MacDonald soon moved his family to Fort Defiance, Arizona.

MacDonald had hoped he could accomplish his aims for the tribe in a single year, but when he arrived at the reservation and saw the severity of the problems there, he realized it would take much longer. Conditions at the reservation were abysmal. MacDonald wrote in *The Last Warrior,* "What I found when I returned was so shocking, so much a continuation of the injustices of the past, that

I would not leave again. I had to radically change the course of my life, my hopes and dreams for the future, in order to do whatever was possible to right the injustices that had become a way of life for the Navajo Nation." Meanwhile, his wife, Ruby, was dismayed to learn that she had to raise two children on his new salary of $13,000 a year in a town where the grocery stores—still called trading posts—often marked up their goods by as much as 120 percent.

MacDonald set to work with fierce determination. It was 1964, and Congress had just passed into law the Economic Opportunity Act, the first step in President Lyndon B. Johnson's War on Poverty. MacDonald sensed that Johnson's new program would bring with it a shift

Native American children play outside their dilapidated home in the late 1960s. On returning to the Navajo reservation in 1963, MacDonald was shocked to find families like this one facing the burdens of unemployment, poor health and education facilities, and ill treatment by government agencies.

in the government's relations with the Native American population. As he put it, "It was the beginning of a new era in government attitude. Washington finally had handed the reins to the Indians and said, 'You drive.' "

Indeed, Sargent Shriver, director of the Office of Economic Opportunity, disagreed with the common wisdom that Indians were incapable of handling their own funds. During his first year in office, he decided to allow 16 tribes to make their own grant proposals rather than receive their funding through the BIA.

MacDonald, at that time director of the tribe's Management Methods and Procedures Department, requested funds for a preschool program, a job-training program, housing loans for low-income families, college scholarships, and a start-up program for a community college. Shriver approved the request and the Navajos were given a grant of $900,000. This money was used to finance the newly formed Office of Navajo Economic Opportunity (ONEO), which would administer the prospective public programs.

A few months later, in 1965, an appreciative Chairman Nakai appointed MacDonald director of the ONEO. MacDonald's first move as head of this office was to make sure it would operate without interference from the Bureau of Indian Affairs, insisting that all federal money for the Navajos be given directly to the ONEO, not to federal bureaucrats. As MacDonald put it in a Tribal Council report, "ONEO was born a Navajo! From the start, as an organization with a 98% Navajo staff, and a Navajo director, it understood its people, and it cared about them."

In his first two years at the helm of the ONEO, MacDonald organized a $12 million antipoverty program. In 1967 he founded Dinébeiina Nahiilna Be Agaditahe (Navajo for "attorneys who contribute to the economic

revitalization of the people"), or DNA, to provide tribe members with free legal services. Within a few months of its creation, DNA had handled 250 cases, and within a year its lawyers were interviewing as many as 100 clients a day, helping them with legal matters ranging from divorce suits to landlord-tenant disputes to grazing rights feuds.

It was during this period that MacDonald's marriage dissolved, and Ruby and their two children, Rocky and Linda, returned to California. Soon afterward, MacDonald married his assistant, a Navajo woman who had helped him implement many programs on the reservation. Over the next few years, Wanda MacDonald became the mother of three daughters, Faith, Hope, and Charity, and she continued to travel with her husband and help him carry out his duties.

Peter MacDonald (third from left) and colleagues gather below the sandstone ridge that marks Window Rock, Arizona. Standing next to MacDonald is his assistant, Wanda LeClere, whom he later married.

There was still much to be done. The Navajo population was increasing at twice the rate as the white population, and this growth placed a heavy burden on the tribe's fragile economy. Meanwhile, more than 80 percent of the businesses on the reservation were owned by non-Indians, and most of them charged their customers exorbitant prices. In order to buy goods or services at competitive rates, the Navajos were forced to drive many miles to off-reservation cities. There was little industry on the reservation and no real business community, and the Navajos continued to make their living from subsistence farming, handicrafts, and tourism.

Despite these harsh conditions, most Navajos chose to stay on the reservation rather than seek work elsewhere. The Navajo religion, history, and clan system all served to bind them to their homelands, and they preferred their own way of life, no matter how impoverished it might be. To meet the competing needs of the Navajo people, Peter MacDonald hoped to improve Navajo life while preserving its distinctiveness. He wanted to introduce the Navajos to mainstream society, where they would be able to find jobs and earn more money, yet he also wanted the tribe to be able to retain its culture and values.

MacDonald knew that some aspects of Navajo culture made it difficult for tribe members to adapt to business as it was conducted in the non-Indian world. One of these was the Navajos' sense of clan obligation. In his book *Red Capitalism*, Kent Gilbreath explains that the Navajos' pastoral, seminomadic way of life has created such strong emotional and economic interdependency within the clans that an individual Navajo's behavior at work is often governed by his or her ties to extended family. For instance, a Navajo businesswoman knows that if she denies a family member credit at her store, she will be ostracized by her clan, so she is likely to extend the credit even if doing so is a risk to her business. Many Navajo businesses have gone bankrupt as a result of the clash between the profit motive and family obligation. Navajo society also tends to look down on individuals who accumulate large amounts of money or property. A rich man may be seen as neglecting his family or accused of stealing from the dead. "The Navajo way is the middle way" is a common aphorism conveying the tribe's respect for moderation. Although they are hardworking and self-disciplined, the Navajos do not, as a culture, value work for its own sake; there is no Navajo equivalent of the Protestant work ethic encouraging individualism and entrepreneurship. White business owners have traditionally interpreted these cultural traits as laziness and imprudence and avoided hiring Indian workers.

In response to these problems, Peter MacDonald hoped to make the Navajo reservation self-sufficient. One of his basic plans was to use ONEO funds to train unemployed men and women as carpenters. The Navajo government would then use other funds to hire the trainees to build low-income reservation housing. The work would be done by Navajos for Navajos, with funding provided by the Navajo government, and everyone would gain business experience in the process.

As head of the ONEO, MacDonald also hoped to renegotiate certain energy leases that the tribe was offering to coal, natural gas, and oil companies, but he lacked the authority to do so. Meanwhile, Chairman Nakai allowed the BIA to negotiate away hundreds of thousands of Navajo acres to multinational coal companies. Nakai, unfamiliar with the intricacies of big business, settled for royalties as low as 15 cents a ton for coal worth 10 times that amount on the open market.

Disappointed in Nakai's mismanagement of Navajo resources, in 1970 MacDonald decided to challenge the chairman in his bid for a third term. MacDonald was by

Newly elected chairman Peter MacDonald talks with Tribal Council member Annie Wauneka in November 1970.

this time well known and generally admired. His portrait hung in the waiting room of ONEO offices across the reservation, and he was able to move easily from managing tribal welfare payments to commanding the loyalty of a large and grateful constituency.

MacDonald selected Wilson Skeet, a Navajo who lived off-reservation, as his running mate. His campaign speeches stressed his concern for preserving land resources while developing enterprise. He pointed to factionalism and corruption in Nakai's government, accused Nakai of subservience to the BIA, and ridiculed the chairman's business sense. MacDonald's claims apparently made a deep impression on Navajo voters; he won by a landslide.

In his January 1971 inaugural address, MacDonald outlined the goals of his administration:

First, what is rightfully ours, we must protect; what is rightfully due us we must claim. Second, what we depend on from others, we must replace with the labor of our own hands and the skills of our own people. Third, what we do not have, we must bring into being. We must create for ourselves.

MacDonald promised to think of the long term—of "our children and their children after them"—when planning for the future and when negotiating deals with big business or the federal government. Finally, he promised Navajo self-sufficiency and self-determination: "We must do it better. We must do it in our own way. And we must do it now."

MacDonald's philosophy quickly became action. No sooner had he taken office than he issued an ultimatum

Sheltering her young daughter from the cold, a Navajo woman watches Peter MacDonald being sworn in as tribal chairman. Some 6,000 Navajos attended the January 1971 inauguration ceremony.

to the BIA: the tribe must have exclusive title to the building that housed the tribal chambers—the same building in which, seven years earlier, he had watched a BIA official chastise two members of the Tribal Council. When the BIA balked, MacDonald threatened to hold all Tribal Council meetings on the building's front steps. The BIA submitted, and MacDonald promptly had the building's locks changed.

But that was only the beginning. Presiding over a meeting of the Navajo Tribal Council, MacDonald scornfully singled out the one BIA official in attendance. "If I hear any outbursts from you or your staff," he warned the man, "I will have our police escort you from these chambers. And you won't be let back in until you promise to behave like an adult!"

This was a turning point for the Navajos and for Peter MacDonald. The federal government had given up its control over the Navajo people. The chairman, meanwhile, had tasted power. In days to come he would challenge the very limits of his authority.

4

THE EMERGING
NAVAJO NATION

The landscape of the Navajo reservation is one of the most dramatic anywhere in the United States. Within its borders are the red-orange sandstone buttes of Monument Valley, the sheer walls, thousands of feet deep, of Canyon de Chelly National Monument, and the green cotton-woods and olives of the desert badlands. In the overhangs of the canyon walls are Anasazi (Navajo for "Ancient Ones") cliff dwellings dating from 350 to 1300 A.D. The impressive crag known as Window Rock dominates the city of that name, center of the Navajo government. It was in the shadow of this natural landmark that Peter MacDonald began his first term as chairman of the Navajo Nation.

Soon after the election, Navajo historian Peter Iverson spoke with a BIA official. Commenting on MacDonald's campaign rhetoric, the agent scoffed at the idea of Navajo self-determination. "[The Navajos] have no economy," he said. "They're utterly dependent on government. How in hell can you talk about it? Self-determination must mean being able to spend the white man's money without accounting for it." This was a bitter evaluation of MacDonald's campaign promises, which combined ideas

Peter MacDonald addresses Washington officials in 1972. During his first term as tribal chairman, MacDonald petitioned the U.S. government for a reorganization of the Bureau of Indian Affairs.

51

of Navajo independence and an increase in the use of government funds.

The new chairman saw it differently. In an ONEO report, MacDonald asserted that "the people must strive toward self-sufficiency, . . . they must become employable, . . . [and] they must be brought up to today's requirements of technology and education." The more funds he could wrest from the federal government to help people gain the skills to be self-determining and employable, he believed, the sooner Navajo country would become an independent nation within the larger nation of the United States.

MacDonald also believed that the Navajos had to make the most of their land, their mineral and energy resources, and their labor force while they developed a better relationship with the non-Indian business world. To these

The Ned A. Hatathli Culture Center is the centerpiece of Navajo Community College, which opened on its permanent campus in 1973. The school was one of the projects of the Navajo Division of Education, created by the Tribal Council during MacDonald's administration.

ends he negotiated with the AFL-CIO, the country's most powerful labor organization, which agreed to provide training to hundreds of workers on the reservation. He also persuaded two large corporations to build factories in Navajo country.

In 1971, MacDonald orchestrated the first-ever Navajo sale of uranium, a radioactive ore used in the production of nuclear power, for $3 million. Another $6 million came into the tribal funds when Exxon bought exploration rights to land near the New Mexico border. MacDonald saw these sales as the beginning of a new era in the use of Navajo resources. Nakai had leased mineral rights to Peabody Coal Company as early as the mid-1960s, but that business deal had ended in disaster: Peabody's strip-mining operations at Black Mesa, New Mexico, had dispossessed the mesa's inhabitants and ruined its ecology. (Strip-mining is a process in which the top layers of earth are stripped away to get at the minerals underneath.) In contrast, the underground mine planned by Exxon Corporation would displace neither people nor livestock.

MacDonald's vision also included widespread reforms in Navajo education. With his encouragement, the Tribal Council approved the creation of the Navajo Division of Education in 1971. This assembly soon garnered funds for the construction of Navajo Community College. In 1973, the division presented proposals for an autonomous Navajo school system, a Navajo teacher-education program, arrangements for bilingual education, a continuing education program, and educational assistance for high school dropouts, all to be supported by federal and tribal funds.

According to Iverson, the chairman's good business sense and his skill at the negotiation table quickly affected the Navajo economy for the better. MacDonald knew that the leases drawn up by the BIA under Nakai's chairmanship had proved largely unprofitable for the tribe. He decided to negotiate new leases that would reflect the market value of Navajo resources, remarking, "It must be clearly understood that it will no longer be accepted practice to sell the reservation off by the ton or by the barrel."

In the critical area of water rights, MacDonald announced that the Navajos would act aggressively to obtain the water they needed to irrigate the arid soil of their reservation. In the mid-1970s, the Navajos became involved in a dispute over their use of the San Juan River, a water source they shared with New Mexico's Four Corners Power Plant. The state of New Mexico had tried to introduce legislation that would limit the Navajos' use of the river. Similarly, Arizona had passed a law that would regulate the Indians' access to the Little Colorado River.

At MacDonald's behest, the Navajo Nation filed suit against New Mexico and Arizona. To ensure that his people would have every advantage in the hearing, MacDonald hired a former federal judge from New York, Simon Rifkin, to represent the tribe, instructing the Tribal Council to pay his exorbitant fees. "We have to have the best," he told the council. "If we are to retain our culture and remain as a tribal entity on our traditional lands, we must make a rapid transition to a modern agricultural and industrial economy. And to do so, we need our share of the water." Rifkin's preparation for the suit so intimidated New Mexico officials that they asked to have the trial postponed—the legislation against the Navajos, meanwhile, fell by the wayside.

During MacDonald's first term, the Navajos became involved with national politics as never before. The chairman even advised the federal government to reorganize the Bureau of Indian Affairs. The BIA was administered by the Department of the Interior, which also housed the Bureau of Reclamation, an office that oversaw the construction and maintenance of dams and other large-scale water projects—projects that could harm the lands of the Navajo reservation. MacDonald argued that the BIA should become an independent agency so that its decisions would be less subject to conflicts of interest. He also demanded that the BIA change its mode of operation. BIA officials who administered the Navajo reservation, he believed, should speak Navajo, be familiar with the Navajo culture, and understand that their job was to serve the Navajos, rather than "regard Indian people and Indian governments much in the way that an overbearing parent regards a recalcitrant child."

Inspired by their new chairman's vehemence, more and more Navajos registered to vote. In Apache County, Arizona, Navajo voters suddenly outnumbered non-Indian voters, drastically affecting the outcome of the 1974 election, when Democrat Raul Castro beat the Republican incumbent for governor. Republican senator Barry Goldwater was reportedly incensed by the outcome of this race. He accused the Navajos of selling out to the AFL-CIO, a traditionally Democratic union. This rift in the Navajos' relationship with the Republican party would have fateful consequences during MacDonald's second term as chairman.

In the 1974 elections, MacDonald easily defeated challengers Raymond Nakai, Charlie Toledo, and Leo Watchman. Despite the efforts of Nakai, who accused MacDonald of trying to turn the Tribal Council into an Anglo-style government, MacDonald and Wilson Skeet were granted almost 70 percent of the vote in an election with the highest voter turnout in Navajo history.

"The theme of this second administration will be 'the emerging Navajo Nation,' " MacDonald told the crowd

attending his 1975 inauguration. "During these next four years we will continue the program we have begun to fully develop the Navajo Nation as an important economic, social and political force in the Southwest and in the United States." MacDonald's inaugural address also contained a warning to the BIA and the U.S. government. "We will neither be patronized nor insulted," he told his audience. "We will be treated as human beings, as members of the proud Navajo Tribe, and as citizens of the United States."

But Senator Barry Goldwater paid no attention to MacDonald's claims. In February 1976 he demanded that the U.S. General Accounting Office audit the Navajo tribe's finances, and the investigation uncovered a $13.3 million kickback scheme devised by the Navajo Housing Authority (NHA) office. Two of the three men who were indicted for the scheme were later cleared of charges, but it was apparent that the NHA had committed serious

Former Arizona senator Barry Goldwater delivers a fiery speech at the 1984 Republican National Convention. Goldwater began reproaching the Navajo Nation in 1974, when Navajo voters helped elect Democratic governor Raul Castro.

offenses, and scandalous rumors about MacDonald's government began to circulate.

In May, several hundred Navajos calling themselves "Navajo People Concerned for Their Government," led by the director of DNA, Peterson Zah, demonstrated for reform at the Navajo Tribal Council chambers. Several months later, a federal grand jury in Phoenix served MacDonald with an eight-count indictment for fraud and tax evasion. MacDonald had allegedly submitted false travel vouchers to the Tucson Gas & Electric Company, a firm that, with MacDonald's support, was planning to extend a power line across the reservation. Appearing in the wake of the NHA hearings, MacDonald's indictment created a stir throughout the Southwest, earning him the nicknames Peter MacDollars and the Navajo Nixon.

George Vlassis, MacDonald's legal adviser, decided that the chairman needed a powerful advocate, and he con-

Native American leaders joined MacDonald at the Tribal Council chambers in 1971 to support his demand for a reorganization of the BIA. MacDonald argued that the BIA should be removed from the control of the Department of the Interior and staffed with agents familiar with Indian culture.

tacted lawyer F. Lee Bailey, who had just completed his defense of the celebrated kidnap victim–turned–terrorist, Patty Hearst. The trial began on May 10, 1977. The Tribal Council, which had passed a formal resolution supporting the chairman, testified on his behalf, and Bailey made the most of inconsistencies in the government's claims. The result was a hung jury and MacDonald's acquittal. Facing the press, a relieved chairman said, "I am happy that when difficulty afflicts us, we still have the strength and determination to prevail."

The effects of the trial were far-reaching. Arguing that his indictment was an attack on all Navajo people, MacDonald proposed that $70,000 be appropriated from the tribal budget to pay his legal fees. The chairman's request was approved, but soon afterward four dissenting council members filed suit against him in the Navajo court for mismanaging tribal funds. The court ruled against MacDonald. From this point on there was a schism within the government that would not be healed.

Meanwhile, MacDonald's plans for reorganizing the tribal government lay forgotten, and deals with off-reservation businesses to build stores and factories on the reservation remained on hold. With so many factors weighing against him, MacDonald seemed an unlikely candidate for a third term as tribal chairman, but he entered the 1978 race with confidence. Challenged by Raymond Nakai, Taylor MacKenzie, James Atcitty, and his own vice-chairman, Wilson Skeet, MacDonald delivered campaign speeches emphasizing his expertise in negotiating energy deals and promising huge increases in tribal funds from prospective leases of uranium and coal.

The incumbent's competitors divided the opposing vote, and MacDonald won the November election with a 3 to 1 margin, becoming the first Navajo chairman in history to win a third term. Having overcome a federal indictment and a difficult campaign, MacDonald was now ready to orchestrate one of the most powerful Native American alliances ever to play a role in the nation's economy: an intertribal organization known as the Council of Energy Resource Tribes.

5

THE NAVAJO SHAH

What are the two things you can still get for 15 cents?" went a Navajo riddle of the 1970s. The answer: "A pack of bubble gum and a ton of Indian coal."

By the mid-1970s, many Navajos were aware that their reservation held uranium and coal deposits worth billions of dollars. Unfortunately, in the 1960s Raymond Nakai and the BIA had leased hundreds of thousands of Navajo acres to coal companies at rates drastically lower than their market value, and few Navajos had enjoyed the benefits of their vast resources. Worse yet, once the coal companies had obtained the use of Navajo lands, they had promptly strip-mined the areas, ravaging some of the most beautiful and ecologically delicate areas in the Southwest.

Hoping to correct these problems, Peter MacDonald began reviewing and renegotiating the Navajos' energy leases during his first term as tribal chairman. In 1974, he met with 20 other tribal leaders in Washington, D.C., to discuss the current market for coal and uranium. From this meeting emerged the Council of Energy Resource Tribes (CERT), an organization whose aims were to negotiate mineral and fuel rights on terms favorable to Native Americans.

CERT's goals, outlined by Peter MacDonald in the

MacDonald visits a coal-mining site on the Navajo reservation. As head of the Council of Energy Resource Tribes, MacDonald sought to ensure that energy companies dealt fairly with Navajos and other Native Americans.

American Indian Journal in 1979, were fourfold. First, the 25 member tribes would inventory their resource holdings, because, explained MacDonald, "You cannot possibly project how you're going to manage or develop the energies that you have unless you know how much you have, where it is, what the quality is, and what the market is." Second, CERT would bring specialists in to guide the Indians through important negotiations. The chairman explained, "You have to buy expertise to sit on the side of the Indian tribes, across the table from energy companies who have years and years of study and research, along with about five or ten lawyers who just specialize in those areas, along with their geologists and engineers. And in the past we've been sitting . . . across from them with some BIA ranch-rider . . . in league with the utilities or energy companies." CERT, he said, would make sure the Indians had their own panel of experts to help them negotiate with energy companies. Third, CERT would find out what the market was for energy resources, "right now, for the next 10 years, and for the next 25 years." And fourth, CERT would encourage young Native Americans to enter such energy-related fields as petroleum engineering, civil engineering, metallurgy, and geology, offering scholarships and internships to members of the 25 tribes so that they could learn "every skill that has to do with minerals."

To fund these projects, CERT turned to the very entity whose authority they were attempting to defy—the federal government. Not surprisingly, the government denied them assistance. But MacDonald would not be dissuaded. Working through federal government channels, he cannily secured a meeting with Ahmand Kooros, Iran's former energy minister. Soon after this encounter, Kooros attended a conference with American energy executives and warned them that they would soon be "dealing with an OPEC-type cartel right within their own borders." (OPEC stands for Organization of the Petroleum Exporting Countries, an organization of Arab oil-producing nations formed to manipulate energy prices.) CERT was suddenly taken seriously, and MacDonald earned himself another of his many nicknames: Shah of the Navajos.

Making an abrupt about-face, the BIA and the Economic Development Administration granted CERT $100,000 in 1977. In 1978, CERT was awarded $2 million to open a Denver office and provide its tribes with technical services and educational programs in energy-related fields. Over time, many government officials came to regard CERT as the "real" authority on Native American resources and to give its assessments equal weight with those of the BIA.

Wearing a traditional velvet shirt and silver and torquoise jewelry, MacDonald enters his third term as tribal chairman.

Encouraged by his success in these areas, MacDonald soon demanded that the federal government recognize the sovereignty of tribal governments by treating them like states: granting them the same responsibilities, the same support, and the same tax privileges. These demands were not heeded, but they impressed the business world. By the end of the 1970s, it was clear that the chairman of CERT and the largest Native American tribe in the United States exercised considerable power outside the Navajo Nation.

CERT became especially active in the politics of the Southwest. The cities of Las Vegas, Los Angeles, San Diego, Phoenix, Tucson, and Albuquerque relied heavily on such Navajo-dependent resources as the Four Corners Power Plant, the largest coal-fired power plant in the world.

As chairman of CERT, MacDonald also indirectly controlled the resources owned by the other member tribes—estimated by the Department of the Interior as comprising 11 percent of all the coal reserves in the nation; 30 percent of all low-sulfur coal west of the Mississippi River suitable for strip-mining; between 40 and 50 percent of all privately owned uranium; 4 percent of the oil and natural gas reserves; and a large share of the nation's oil shale and geothermal resources. In his book *Now That the Buffalo's Gone,* a discussion of modern Indian-white relations, Historian Alvin M. Josephy, Jr., claims that CERT was "the most relevant Indian voice" of the 1970s and 1980s.

MacDonald's influence on the outside world was very much in evidence on March 1, 1981, when several hundred leading industrialists, insurance company executives, energy conglomerate board members, bankers, and Wall Street investment house partners joined CERT members and tribal leaders at a black-tie dinner at the

In 1982, MacDonald attended a celebration of Indian business ventures at the Kennedy Center in Washington, D.C. Later he presented President Ronald Reagan with this gift from the Navajo people, a handwoven rug representing the American flag.

Pierre Hotel in New York City. The Navajo chairman was guest speaker. As he stood to address an audience who had paid $1,000 a plate for the privilege of hearing him talk, he showed no signs of nervousness. MacDonald told the crowd:

> I sense that one day energy projects on CERT-member lands shall be singled out by the rest of the world as models for how development can occur in a manner which respects the natural and cultural environment as well. That is how it must be—for real "progress," in the view of my people, must transcend profits. It must outlast generations. It must help us realize a vision articulated by Chief Joseph of the Nez Perces a century ago: "Let me be a free man—free to travel, free to stop, free to work, free to trade where I choose, free to choose my own teachers, free to follow the religion of my fathers, free to think and act and talk for myself. . . . For this time, the Indian race are waiting and praying."

A year later, the new partnership between tribal chairmen and industrialists was again celebrated, this time at the Kennedy Center in Washington, D.C., where the Night of the First Americans was attended by President Ronald Reagan and a host of government, business, and social leaders. Box seats for this extravaganza sold for $5,000 apiece.

Among the Navajos, Peter MacDonald's high profile in the business world prompted not only pride but also deep misgivings. Many of the Indians were afraid that their chairman was taking them into the industrialized world too quickly; others did not believe the tribe should be entering that world at all. MacDonald had a pragmatic view of 20th-century Native American culture. He told the *American Indian Journal*: "I don't think culture is living in a hogan, running around in a breechcloth and sitting by a stream looking at the stars. Culture is in the soul, in the spirit. The Navajo went from the horse to the pickup truck. Now the pickup truck is part of Navajo culture." But many traditionalists and environmentalists feared that, along with the pickup truck, Navajo culture now meant the shopping center, the strip mine, the power plant, and radioactive pollution.

Respected novelist and environmentalist Peter Matthiessen, describing a 1979 tour of the Navajo reservation in his book *Indian Country*, was horrified by the results of MacDonald's multimillion-dollar energy deals. The area's power plants, he noted, had filled the air with an "unseen mist of lead, mercury dioxides, sulphuric acid, and other sickening pollutants."

To illustrate the risks uranium mining posed to both Native Americans and their land, Matthiessen describes the mining operations headed by Kerr-McGee, who in 1948 became the first company to extract uranium from Navajo lands. To reduce costs, the company hired Navajos unfamiliar with the dangers of radioactive substances, sending them into the mines without protective masks or any warning of the dangers their work entailed. No drinking water was available for the miners, so they often drank from radioactive puddles on the mine floor. Not surprisingly, within a few years of the mine's closing, one miner in five had died either of anaplastic cancer of the lungs or pulmonary fibrosis, a disease contracted from breathing dust over an extended period of time. When Kerr-McGee denied responsibility for the miners' deaths and closed the mine, they left behind, in Matthiessen's estimation, "a poisoned and poverty-stricken community, a radioactive mill, and seventy-one acres of spent uranium ore that is estimated to retain up to eighty-five percent of the original radiation. These 'tailings,' exposed to wind and rain, were dumped about twenty yards from the banks of the San Juan River, the crucial source of water for the region."

Ultimately, Native American traditionalists came to view CERT less as a champion of self-determination than as a threat to their culture and environment. This skepticism increased as CERT's ties to such powerful oil companies as Arco, Exxon, and Gulf became known. In 1981, four major tribes seceded from the organization, fearing that MacDonald would force them into uranium mining deals with energy consortiums.

Some of the most fervent opposition to Peter MacDonald's energy deals came from the members of the American Indian Movement (AIM). "Peter MacDollars *is* the shah of the Navajo," AIM cofounder Russell Means told *Mother Jones* in 1979. "I pity him. He's a victim of the industrial society." AIM opposed the mining of Indian lands on moral grounds, believing that such operations constituted a violation of the living earth. The group even denied the authority of the tribal councils, which, according to Means, were formed by the BIA in violation of more traditional forms of democratic government.

Russell Means, cofounder of the American Indian Movement (AIM), speaks at a 1987 news conference. Means and other members of AIM opposed MacDonald, whose mining contracts, they believed, led to the destruction of Indian lands.

AIM and MacDonald had not always held such widely diverging views. In 1972, MacDonald had supported the AIM takeover of the Washington, D.C., BIA building, telling viewers on television's *Face the Nation* that AIM's actions reflected the "rage and frustration all Indian people feel." In 1975, with some reluctance, he had even supported the AIM occupation of Fairchild Semiconductor, a company based in Shiprock, New Mexico, that had laid off many of its Navajo employees after they tried to form a union. The takeover was settled peaceably, but Fairchild closed soon after, moving its operations to a cheap-labor area in Latin America, and AIM and MacDonald were blamed for the resulting unemployment. From that point on, the pragmatic MacDonald had valued jobs more than political idealism, and AIM— whose spiritual conception of Mother Earth was probably bound to conflict with the chairman's ambitions in any case—had staunchly opposed him.

In the late 1970s, AIM asserted that the rich deals negotiated by CERT had never benefited anyone beyond the tribal councils. The group also noted that, despite MacDonald's reputation as a fierce negotiator, in 1975 the Navajos were paid 60 cents a pound for uranium ore that sold for twice that amount commercially.

AIM was not MacDonald's only critic. According to Peter Matthiessen, many Navajos took a dim view of MacDonald's "white" habits, which included traveling by Learjet and Lincoln Continental. Some Navajos reported that the chairman employed a pair of male witches who used "bad medicine" against anyone who opposed his plans. "The Chairman controls everything—the council, the courts, the committees, the police," remarked one Tribal Council representative. "He's more interested in mining than people."

MacDonald continued to insist that the sale of Navajo resources would benefit the tribe as a whole. In 1979 he told *American Indian Journal*: "If we develop our resources in the context of our own culture, within our own time span, and with respect to those things that the Navajos have a great deal of concern for like environment and home life, . . . I think energy development can be managed in such a way that it will assist the tribe to move forward and to survive."

In 1976, 700,000 acres of Indian land—the greater part

of which was Navajo—was leased to mining companies for exploration or excavation. Most of these leases were negotiated by the BIA without the participation of Native American leaders. CERT's power notwithstanding, Mac-Donald spent much of his second term struggling to gain control of his own tribe's natural resources.

Then tragedy struck the Navajo Nation. On July 16, 1979, a decayed dam at a United Nuclear Corporation tailings millpond in Church Rock, New Mexico, gave way, and 94 million gallons of radioactive water gushed into the Rio Puerco, causing what the Nuclear Regulatory Commission termed the worst contamination in the history of the nuclear industry. Although the BIA had negotiated the United Nuclear Corporation's lease in 1978 without Navajo participation, in 1981 a federal district

Native American protesters speak with an official during their 1975 takeover of Fairchild Semiconductor, a factory in Shiprock, New Mexico. AIM sponsored the demonstration after the company laid off Navajo employees seeking higher pay and better working conditions.

court ruling prevented the Navajos from suing the corporation in Navajo court, on the grounds that Navajo jurisdiction "conflicts with the superior federal interest in regulating the production of nuclear power." This betrayal on the part of the U.S. government reflected badly on Peter MacDonald, who had always prided himself on his close ties with the administration of President Ronald Reagan.

Meanwhile, the Navajo government bureaucracy continued to grow. As the Navajo people struggled with unemployment, illiteracy, and alcoholism, the budget of the Tribal Council increased from $18 million to $137 million. In 1981, MacDonald backed a resolution that granted the chairman a lifetime pension of $55,000 a year and increased the salaries of council members from the 1973 level of $7,000 a year to $20,000 a year—more than 20 times what the average reservation-dweller earned. Despite widespread resentment toward his use of tribal funds, MacDonald hired a $1.5-million Hollywood publicist to handle the tribe's public relations and an expensive New York lawyer to oversee contract negotiations.

With the 1982 election approaching, many of MacDonald's onetime supporters were seeking leadership elsewhere. Some Navajo voters hoped to find a more traditional "middle way" in the candidacy of Peterson Zah. Others found themselves agreeing with the more radical AIM, which resisted not only the federal government but also the Navajo Tribal Council and the whole system of leadership directing the future of the Navajo Nation.

6

▼▽▼▽▼▽

BIG MOUNTAIN
AND "BO-GATE"

On October 28, 1979, a community of Navajo Indians who lived in and around a place called Big Mountain, in the northern desert of Arizona, issued a declaration of independence from the United States, the state of Arizona, and the jurisdiction of the Navajo Tribal Council. This act of secession was precipitated by the passage of U.S. Public Law 93-531, which required some 6,000 Navajos to give up their homes in an area they had occupied jointly with the Hopis since 1882. Many of the people affected by the law were very like Peter MacDonald's own parents and grandparents—traditional Native Americans whose self-sufficient lifestyle revolved around their farms and ranches. Few of the area's inhabitants spoke English or had ever held a paying job.

Acting as an advocate for the Big Mountain Navajos, MacDonald blamed "restrictive government policies" for confining the Navajos and Hopis to reservations in the first place. In the foreword to *No Place to Go*, anthropologist Thayer Scudder's study of the relocation program, MacDonald wrote:

> It is clear that the government . . . has only succeeded in compounding the errors of the last century. . . . For the typi-

A resident of Big Mountain, Arizona, cuts the wire fence separating Hopi and Navajo lands in a 1986 demonstration against U.S. Public Law 93-531. The law required some 6,000 Navajos to leave an area they had traditionally shared with the Hopis.

cal Navajo relocatee, who has lived all his life in the free and open lands of the Navajo nation, this banishment . . . constitutes little more than a spiritual death sentence.

MacDonald's claim was no exaggeration. Rates of sickness, alcoholism, depression, and suicide were extraordinarily high among those Indians who had already followed the government order and left their lands. Many Navajos were calling the relocation, which was projected to cost U.S. taxpayers $1 billion, the Second Long Walk.

Some 400 Navajo families were resisting the government order to vacate the joint-use area. Some of these people believed that the Navajo Tribal Council had betrayed them, and that the purpose of the relocation was

Realizing that they must leave their homes in the joint-use area, Navajos weep during a meeting in Cactus Valley, Arizona. "In our tongue," said one woman, "there is no word for relocation. To move away means to disappear and never be seen again."

to make way for large-scale ranching, coal mining, and uranium extraction in the area. "There's no dispute between the Navajo and Hopi," Hopi elder Thomas Banyacya told ecologist Jerry Mander, who reported the statement in his book *In the Absence of the Sacred.* "It's the Tribal Councils and the big energy companies and the U.S. government who are in dispute against the Navajo and Hopi who live on the land."

Meanwhile, many Navajos continued to blame MacDonald for igniting the wrath of Senator Goldwater, who championed the Hopis' claims in Congress. Emily Benedek explores the troubled relationship between MacDonald and Goldwater in her history of the Navajo-Hopi land dispute, *The Wind Won't Know Me.* During Mac-Donald's first term as tribal chairman, Goldwater had hesitated to support the Navajos in their fight for the joint-use area, and MacDonald had tried to use political leverage to gain the senator's backing. In 1972, the chairman, a registered Republican, announced that if Goldwater refused to defend the Navajos, he would desert the Republican party in the upcoming presidential elections and support Democrat George McGovern, who had publicly pledged his opposition to the relocation. According to Wayne Sekaquaptewa, publisher of the Hopi newspaper, MacDonald's ploy had so angered Goldwater that the senator had sided with the Navajos' opponents from that point on.

The relocation order sparked so much protest that eventually the Indians were given an opportunity to work out an alternative plan. In June 1982, representatives of the Navajo and Hopi tribes, including MacDonald and his legal adviser George Vlassis, agreed to meet and renegotiate the relocation framework. The meeting was scheduled to begin at 9:00 A.M. When the clock struck 9, the Hopi representatives and the federal mediator were

MacDonald shakes hands with Hopi chairman Abbott Sekaquaptewa before a meeting on the Navajo-Hopi land dispute. Some critics suspected the leaders of colluding to reach a settlement that would serve their own personal interests.

seated around the council table—but the Navajo coalition was missing. The group waited 15 minutes without a sign from the Navajos; then the Hopis, certain that they were being insulted, adjourned the meeting and went home. A few minutes later, MacDonald and Vlassis arrived at an empty room. The Hopis blamed MacDonald for this fiasco and refused to negotiate with him again.

Soon after this controversy came rumors that the chairmen of the Hopi and Navajo tribes were secretly supporting the relocation for reasons of personal gain. Hopi chairman Abbott Sekaquaptewa, a rancher, was said to have been offered some of the relinquished land; MacDonald was reputed to have ties with Peabody Coal, which hoped to carry out strip-mining operations in the region.

Unfortunately, by 1982 the Navajos had ample reason to believe that MacDonald was abusing the powers of his office. According to *Mother Jones,* during the 1978 election for tribal chairman, MacDonald had caused the name of one of his opponents, Shiprock chapter president Donald Benally, to be dropped from the ballot. Apparently, MacDonald had pressured the Navajo Board of Election Supervisors—a five-member board chosen by the chairman and headed by his administrative aide Raymond Lancer—to declare Benally underage. The board's decision was overturned by the Navajo Tribal Court after Benally filed a suit to protest it.

Frustrated by the Tribal Court's intrusion, MacDonald had drawn up plans for a higher court of eight justices—all of whom were to be personally appointed by the chairman—and imbued it with the authority to overthrow lower court decisions. To this council MacDonald had quickly appointed some close political friends (including his brother-in-law); none of the eight appointees was a lawyer.

The first case brought before the new council was that of Donald Benally. After about an hour of testimony the council overthrew the Tribal Court's decision, and once again Benally's name was removed from the ballot. "It . . . was real scary," a Navajo legal aide told *Mother Jones.* "The rule of law was out the window."

MacDonald's despotic actions had alarmed the Navajo public. Many tribe members spoke of leaving the reservation to live in Arizona, Utah, or New Mexico. "We'd be better off living in the United States," Donald Benally remarked. "We could at least appeal to the district courts for our rights. Here, where is our redress? We have no independent court system, no checks and balances, no due process, no equal protection. One man controls the whole system here."

After receiving death threats, MacDonald had traveled with armed bodyguards. Meanwhile, he persisted in trying to control the Navajo Tribal Court. In December 1978 he removed from the bench two judges who had repeatedly found his demands unlawful and replaced them with jurists who would, in the words of a judiciary committee member, "support the Chairman 100 percent."

By 1982, an election year, MacDonald's popularity was clearly on the wane. And now, for the first time in 12 years, an educated, intelligent, and charismatic leader was ready to oppose him. Peterson Zah, the director of DNA, was respected as a capable and principled administrator. Many Navajos admired his air of quiet strength and

Newly elected chairman Peterson Zah heads for the tribal government offices at Window Rock. Zah's unruffled demeanor and quiet intelligence helped him defeat MacDonald in 1982.

dignity. Others would be swayed by Zah's sophisticated campaign, organized by Claudeen Bates Arthur, the first Navajo woman attorney. Advocating reform on all levels of tribal government, Zah won the election with a comfortable lead.

Humiliated, MacDonald returned to California. Within a few months he was employed as sales and marketing director for Cataract, Inc., a nuclear power instrumentation and controls firm owned by a friend in the Ojibwa tribe. At Cataract, as in Navajo government, MacDonald proved a persuasive deal maker, and his successes were prodigious. When he joined the firm, it was bringing in an annual income of $18 million. Within two years, MacDonald had helped raise that figure to $50 million.

Meanwhile, a national recession, cutbacks in federal aid to Native Americans, and continuing battles between the Navajos and Hopis made life difficult for Peterson Zah. Although the new Hopi chairman, Ivan Sidney, was an old friend of Zah's, the two leaders seemed unable to bring the land dispute to a close. The Navajo and Hopi tribal councils refused to consider any compromises offered by the chairmen, and the continued relocation of Navajo families reflected badly on Zah's abilities as a negotiator.

Whenever MacDonald visited the reservation, he impressed himself on disillusioned Zah supporters as a militant opponent of relocation. Some were struck by the former chairman's obvious success in the business world. With unemployment on the reservation reaching 49 percent, most Navajos longed above all for an end to the tribe's financial troubles, and MacDonald's business experience lent weight to his plans for economic development. When he entered the 1986 race for tribal chairman, voters responded enthusiastically to his rallying cry of "Jobs, jobs, jobs!" MacDonald's return to public favor was soon reflected at the polls. In 1986, Zah's 52-year-old challenger was elected to an unprecedented fourth term by 750 votes.

Not everyone approved of MacDonald's political comeback. The week before his inauguration, the fiercely independent *Navajo Times* reminded readers of the recent past:

> The election of Peter MacDonald has revived an interesting Navajo political debate: Is the Navajo government a government by crony, . . . in which advisers qualify not by experience or talent but by their longtime friendship with the Chief Executive? . . . We wonder, for example, what kind of talent will head the tribe's Washington, D.C., office? Will it be Navajos in the lobbying trenches or expensive law firms and consultants? . . . We fear the latter.

Five weeks after taking office, MacDonald, citing the tribe's budget problems, closed down the *Navajo Times*. When the paper resumed publication a few months later, it was little more than a calendar of events.

With the opposition effectively silenced, the chairman introduced his new probusiness, projobs agenda. MacDonald wanted to stop emphasizing federal aid as a resource for the Navajos' $400-million-a-year budget, and encourage tribe members to start their own businesses instead. He also hoped to persuade outsiders—such as the Japanese—to set up manufacturing plants on the reservation. "Four years on the outside gave me a different perspective," MacDonald explained in *Business Week* in August 1987. "I decided if I had another chance, I would make strong economic development a program for the [Navajo] Nation." Later he commented, "Some tribes encouraged enterprise, but I used to discourage it. We built up a lot of barriers to keep everybody away. Now we're tearing them down."

In the spring of 1987, MacDonald began organizing the first-ever Navajo economic summit. Sponsored by U.S.

senators Pete Domenici and Dennis DeConcini, the two-day meeting would be attended by five senators, four congressmen, three governors, the head of the Bureau of Indian Affairs, several tribal officials, and executives from major corporations. President Reagan was to deliver a special message by videotape. It was to be the crowning achievement of MacDonald's long political career.

On July 24, 1987, the opening day of the summit, MacDonald told his audience:

> I ask you all to imagine for a moment what it is like for a young Navajo to pick up a newspaper or turn on the evening news. It is the feeling of being America's economic orphan. It is the anger of asking why the forces of risk and reward, which have built the most robust economic engine on earth, have passed us by. It is the despair of fearing to dream great dreams, lest they never come to pass.

MacDonald's appeal did not go unheard. A few months

MacDonald confers with U.S. senator Pete Domenici (right) during the 1987 Navajo economic summit. In the background is another sponsor of the meeting, Senator Dennis DeConcini.

later, MacDonald appeared before the National Press Club to announce a joint venture with the fashion designer Oleg Cassini, one of the business luminaries who had attended the summit. Cassini intended to license his fashion and jewelry designs for Navajo manufacture. He also planned to help the tribe build a luxury resort that would exploit the natural beauty of their reservation. "There is only one Grand Canyon, and we have it," MacDonald told the assembled reporters. "Canyon de Chelly, Monument Valley, the Painted Desert, the Petrified Forest—all these are on Navajo land. But we have never attempted to tap these resources." Given the decade's depressed oil prices and reductions in federal aid, the only way to deal with the crisis in the Navajo economy was to bring jobs to the reservation, MacDonald said. Stressing the Navajo people's adaptability and their capacity for hard work, he added, "I believe the spirit it takes for that is not too different from what you must do to run a service station or a grocery store or several apartments."

Throughout his first year back in office, MacDonald seemed to be working hard for the betterment of his people, and with impressive results. Still, the chairman's longstanding image—that of the tyrant, the spendthrift, and the powermonger—had not been forgotten, and it would not be long before that "other" Peter MacDonald would once again show his face.

In the summer of 1987, Betty Reid, a reporter from the Gallup, New Mexico, *Independent* and a former writer for the *Navajo Times*, received a tip from someone within the Navajo tribal government. The note told her to look at the deed of the Big Boquillas Ranch, a 491,000-acre tract of land west of Flagstaff, Arizona. Reid knew that the Tribal Council had recently decided to buy this ranch to increase the reservation's land holdings.

When she called the county assessor's office, she discovered something very unusual. Apparently the ranch had been purchased on July 9, 1987, at 9:50 A.M. for $26.2 million, then resold to the Navajo Nation at 9:55 A.M. for $33.4 million—bringing in a profit of $7.2 million in just five minutes!

On July 24, 1987, the front page of the Gallup *Independent* announced the opening day of Peter MacDonald's groundbreaking Navajo economic summit. On the same day, in a single column beside the summit story, the paper ran a short piece about the questionable ranch purchase by the Navajo tribe.

As Peter MacDonald stood at the podium and genially welcomed visiting senators to the Navajo economic summit, no one could have known that he was teetering on the precipice of public disgrace. "Bo-Gate," as the Big Boquillas Ranch scandal became known, would soon be the talk of the Navajo Nation and the world.

7

"MUTTON YES! GOLF BALLS NO!"

MacDonald 'Wild' with Tribe Money" ran the headline in the October 6, 1989, Arizona *Daily Sun*. Day after day, headlines such as this one were appearing in newspapers and magazines across the country, alleging the chairman's misuse of tribal funds. According to these sources, bills for a subscription to *True Confessions*, sporting goods, a chartered plane to take MacDonald and his wife to the Rose Bowl, and a trip to his daughter's graduation in Massachusetts were among the $69,286 worth of unpaid office expenses MacDonald had presented to the Navajo Tribal Council.

But extravagant spending was apparently only one of the ways MacDonald had breached the trust of his people. In 1988, investigators found evidence that the chairman was directly involved in an attempt to defraud the Navajo tribe. When Byron "Bud" Brown, a close friend of the chairman's, had bought the Big Boquillas Ranch with oilman Tom Tracy, then sold the ranch five minutes later to the Navajos at a $7.2 million profit, MacDonald had apparently played a major part in the deal.

On November 26, 1989, the *New York Times Magazine* reported that Ninibah Cahn, the director of the Navajo Office of Land Administration, had, at MacDonald's

Peter MacDonald addresses business leaders at the National Press Club in October 1987. The following year, the chairman was investigated for his part in the fraudulent purchase of the Big Boquilllas Ranch.

Members of the Navajo Tribal Council visit the Big Boquillas Ranch before its purchase in July 1987.

request, ordered tribal appraisers to inflate the value of the "Big Bo" from between $50 and $63 an acre to $68 an acre. MacDonald had then arranged for the Navajo tribe to agree to purchase the ranch at the inflated price. His friends Brown and Tracy were to buy the property at its original value just before the Navajo purchase.

The option agreement to buy the ranch was prepared by Stanley M. Pollack, an attorney in the tribe's justice department. "I kept thinking, 'What's the big rush?' " the attorney told *New York Times* reporter Sandy Tolan. Pollack took the contract home to review it before completing the option agreement. That night he got a call from the chairman. "What's the problem?" MacDonald asked him. Pollack began explaining that it was a complicated contract, but he was cut off by MacDonald's curt words: "You know what I want."

Pollack quickly okayed the contract, and Brown and Tracy were given a nonrefundable $500,000 downpayment for the ranch. This transaction made some Navajo officials suspicious, and not long after Reid broke the story about apparent improprieties in the purchase of the "Big Bo," the U.S. government began investigating the deal.

In 1988 a special Senate committee was already conducting hearings on the activities of the BIA, whose officials had been accused of accepting kickbacks from energy companies. By the fall, the committee had begun to focus on Peter MacDonald. A surveillance van monitored the chairman's every move, and his home and office phones were tapped.

What the committee reported was widespread corruption throughout the Navajo tribal government. From 75 to 100 tribal officials were implicated in kickback schemes. Peter MacDonald himself was charged with 111 criminal counts of conspiracy to commit fraud and election tampering. At the top of the list of his misdeeds was the Big Boquillas Ranch "flip-flop."

Bud Brown turned informer for the Senate committee in exchange for immunity from prosecution. He taped a conversation with the chairman in which MacDonald asked both Brown and his own son, Rocky, a lawyer in San Jose, California, to lie in order to hide their transgressions.

Both men later testified against the chairman. Brown informed the committee that he had agreed to pay MacDonald between $500,000 and $750,000 from the profits of the ranch deal, and that MacDonald had already accepted a new BMW automobile and $125,000 in cash. Thirty-six-year-old Rocky MacDonald explained that his

father had used a code whenever he wanted another payment from Brown. "What was that code word?" Ken Ballen, the committee's chief counsel, asked Rocky. "'Golf balls,'" Rocky responded. "A golf ball was approximately $1,000." When the chairman asked him why he participated in the cover-up, Rocky replied, "Because I love my father."

MacDonald refused to testify during the Senate committee hearings on the grounds that he might incriminate himself. Publicly, however, he insisted that racism was at the root of the charges against him. In February 1989, MacDonald broadcast his side of the story on KTNN, the reservation's radio station. "They said they were going to investigate the BIA . . . and yet they lied. Instead they have been investigating me. The reports of the conspiracy—they are lies, my people. This you should remember."

When speaking with non-Indian reporters, MacDonald generally portrayed himself as the victim of persecution by his opponents on the reservation. "Success always brings a certain amount of envy and jealousy," he told *Mother Jones.* "They see me as someone who's close to the public, who's wealthy, as though there's something obscene about wealth. Is it better for them to be wealthy and their leaders not wealthy?"

The national press made the most of the scandal. "Letting Down the Tribe" and "Chief Offender" read the headlines in *Time*; MacDonald's alleged misdeeds were also detailed in *Newsweek, Business Week,* and newspapers around the country.

Some people—Native Americans and non-Indians alike—wondered if the focus of attention on a corrupt Indian leader was the government's attempt to downplay BIA wrongdoing. The *New York Times Magazine* reported that some staff members of the investigating

Peter MacDonald, Jr., testifies before a special Senate committee investigating charges of corruption in the Navajo tribal government. The chairman's son admitted to helping his father cover up a fraudulent transaction in the purchase of the Big Boquillas Ranch.

Senate committee resigned when the committee began investigating MacDonald rather than the BIA. "The chief counsel was only interested in a big hit," a Washington insider told reporter Sandy Tolan. "This was Watergate in Indian country. The media were all primed. But it overshadowed everything else. And it only made the Indians look corrupt."

In October 1989 MacDonald told the *New York Times* that he would "stand up and fight" the allegations. The chairman claimed he had been framed by the federal government because he had advocated Indian rights and denied officials access to the Navajos' natural resources. MacDonald continued to insist that he had never taken kickbacks. "Yes, I have accepted gifts," the 60-year-old chairman said in a broadcast on KTNN. "But that is not a crime." Gifts, he asserted, were part of the Navajo tradition. Besides, whatever he had done did not compare to the excesses of Washington politicians. MacDonald told *Newsweek* that he had already been the object of 186 investigations, from the FBI to the IRS, and he was certain he would weather this one. He even vowed that he would run for re-election in 1990—and win.

In the meantime, MacDonald continued to dominate the Navajo Tribal Council. In February 1989, the 88-member body split into two factions. One faction sought MacDonald's resignation; the other wanted him to remain in office until the 1990 elections. One day the two parties got caught up in a heated debate outside the chairman's office; the council members became so aggravated that they nearly came to blows. According to the *New York Times Magazine,* Daniel Peaches, the tribe's deputy director of legislative affairs, asked MacDonald to do something about the conflict taking place outside his window. "If you allow people to hurt each other, then you've lost control of this whole thing," he told the leader.

MacDonald listens somberly as Tribal Council members decide whether to place him on administrative leave in February 1989.

MacDonald remained seated at his desk. "So be it," he told Peaches. "Let them fight. Let them hurt each other."

On February 17, after four days of bitter disputes in the council chambers, a 49-member majority placed Peter MacDonald on administrative leave. MacDonald gave an emotional farewell speech and received a standing ovation from the council. When the news that he had resigned was announced to the crowd of people waiting outside, they responded with cheers. Many brandished golf balls in their fists and sported buttons declaring, "Mutton Yes! Golf Balls No!"

The Council quickly appointed Marshall Plumber interim chairman. Their choice annoyed MacDonald, who had wanted his vice-chairman, Johnny Thompson, to take on that role. MacDonald was even more unhappy when he was informed that the council had refused his request that the Navajo government pay his legal expenses and provide an office for his defense team. He wrote a memo saying he would not, after all, resign his chairmanship and left a copy of it on each of the councilors' desks.

On February 18, MacDonald's legal adviser, Geoffrey Standingbear, informed the council that Marshall Plumber's appointment was meaningless, as such decisions required approval by two-thirds of the council rather than a simple majority. Because the Navajos have never ratified a constitution, such charges can easily divide the council as members dispute the rules of government, and this is clearly what MacDonald hoped would happen.

On February 21, MacDonald's lawyer obtained a temporary restraining order against the council from Circuit Court Judge Harry Brown—MacDonald's brother-in-law—and MacDonald was reappointed chairman. The Tribal Supreme Court immediately challenged this action. Yet in April, to the nation's surprise, the Tribal Council accepted Judge Brown's ruling. MacDonald offically returned to his role as acting chairman, although he was barred from writing checks on the Navajo treasury. A few days later, the council reversed its decision and fired MacDonald. The governing body was once again stymied by bickering and factionalism.

On April 18, MacDonald's supporters, in protest over the chairman's dismissal, took over his luxurious office and began issuing tribal mandates as MacDonald dictated

Navajo tribal police form a human barrier between MacDonald's supporters and some 500 demonstrators calling for his removal from office.

them over the phone. An interim government issued contradictory mandates from the council chambers. Chaos reigned.

Finally, on May 24, the tribal police, acting on the interim council's orders, forcibly evicted MacDonald's supporters from his office. The calm that followed these events was broken two months later when MacDonald wrote a memo to his former chief of police reappointing him in order to "assist with the orderly restoration . . . of the Navajo Government." It was clear that a coup d'état was in the making.

MacDonald made a series of inflammatory speeches against his opponents, and by mid-July tempers on the reservation were once again running high. On July 20, a group of MacDonald's supporters, armed with baseball bats and wooden stakes, gathered at the tribe's admini- stration and finance building. When a tribal policeman arrived, the crowd tied him up and took away his gun. More policemen appeared on the scene. According to Marley Shebala, a Navajo reporter with the Farmington, New Mexico, *Daily Times*, the crowd began beating the officers with their sticks "in a frenzy." The police fired into the crowd, killing two of MacDonald's supporters as the rest dispersed in confusion.

In October 1989 MacDonald was accused of accepting $157,000 in illegal campaign contributions. His vice- chair, Johnny Thompson, was also charged with violating tribal election laws. Wanda MacDonald was indicted on three criminal counts of receiving kickbacks for her husband, and Rocky MacDonald was charged with taking "consulting" jobs from companies that hoped to make deals with the Navajo tribe and passing the paychecks he received on to his father.

In 1982 MacDonald told *Mother Jones*, "The Anglo world has long lost its honesty and trustworthiness.

Everything is geared to exploitation. If we are to survive, we must understand their crookedness and dishonesty." Many now believed that MacDonald understood Anglo dishonesty all too well.

8

THE LAST WARRIOR

MacDonald speaks to a reporter before beginning his fourth term as tribal chairman. Faced with criminal charges in federal, state, and tribal courts, MacDonald remained preoccupied with legal battles throughout his last two years in office.

When Peter MacDonald was still Hoshkaisith Begay, a fatherless boy growing up in the mountains of Arizona, an incident occurred that would affect him for the rest of his life. Five-year-old Hoshkaisith was herding sheep with his mother one day when his great-uncle Chizsi began yelling his name from a nearby field. The boy was afraid of his great-uncle and refused to answer until his mother prodded him. "Get out in the open," Chizsi shouted. "I'm going to shoot you."

Hoshkaisith's mother pushed him away, and he moved reluctantly into the clearing. Small and alone, he watched as Chizsi raised his rifle, aimed, and fired. Hoshkaisith flinched, then raggedly exhaled; the bullet had come nowhere near him. This, he realized, was his great-uncle's way of instructing him to obey without question. MacDonald recalls this anecdote in his autobiography, *The Last Warrior*, and credits his uncle with teaching him to "prevail over any hardship, to survive any adversity."

MacDonald's boyhood training stood him in good stead

97

through the many hardships and humiliations he faced following his federal indictment for fraud in 1989. Throughout the long ordeal, MacDonald maintained his innocence, calling the criminal charges leveled against him "baloney." Accused in the Arizona state court of attempting to defraud the Navajo Nation of $33.4 million in the Big Boquillas Ranch purchase, and of fraud and election tampering in the Navajo Tribal Court, MacDonald knew he could spend up to 15 years in prison if found guilty.

At the initial state court hearing in Tuba City, MacDonald's lawyer, Joe Keilp, argued that it was "totally unprecedented" for an Indian leader to be tried in both tribal and state courts—but to no avail. Peter MacDonald

MacDonald confers with legal adviser Irwin Bowman in the fall of 1987, shortly after the purchase of the Big Boquillas Ranch. In October 1989 MacDonald appeared before the Navajo tribal court without any form of legal counsel.

was to face three separate trials in state and tribal courts. Keilp decided to give up MacDonald's defense for personal reasons.

Years before, when MacDonald was tried for accepting kickbacks from Tucson Gas & Electric Company, the chairman had hired one of the best lawyers in the country to argue his innocence. On October 30, 1989, however, MacDonald appeared in Window Rock District Tribal Court without any lawyer at all. "I'm still in the process of retaining counsel," he told Judge Robert Yazzie. "I can't find one." Knowing that MacDonald was still drawing his $55,000-a-year salary, Judge Yazzie did not accept MacDonald's claim that he was too poor to afford counsel, and he refused to grant the erstwhile chairman a court-appointed lawyer. Yazzie did, however, allow MacDonald to be released on his own recognizance—a gesture of respect toward the compromised leader.

Undeterred, MacDonald disputed Judge Yazzie's impartiality and requested that he be replaced. MacDonald had once tried to deny Yazzie a permanent judgeship on the Tribal Court, and in March 1989 he had actually dismissed him from the bench. The judge had been reinstated by the interim chairman Leonard Haskie after he won an appeal in the Navajo Supreme Court. Yazzie denied that he would be prejudiced against MacDonald and insisted on hearing his case.

In the fall of 1990, despite an uncertain future, MacDonald threw himself into his sixth re-election campaign. Facing challenger Peterson Zah, MacDonald made speeches from atop a 16-wheeler at a Navajo fair and garnered enough support to pose a serious threat to his opponent. "It's been a long road back from political captivity," he told reporters after he won the October primary, adding that he was looking forward to the November elections.

But October was not yet over. That month, Judge Yazzie presided over the Tribal Court as businessmen who had dealt with MacDonald testified that he had accepted kickbacks while chairman of the Navajo tribe. Mark Donatelli, the tribe's special prosecutor, accused MacDonald of "basically setting up a tollgate for people who wanted to do business on the reservation." Father and son had acted as a team, the prosecutor asserted, soliciting $400,000 in so-called consulting fees and loans from businessmen seeking preferential treatment or lucrative contracts with the tribe.

Facing 45 counts of bribe soliciting, extortion, conspiracy, and ethical misconduct, MacDonald listened impassively to the testimony. His expression remained stern and remote as businessman Lee Hough told the jury that MacDonald had promised his company an exclusive contract to train Navajo workers if he paid Rocky MacDonald $10,000 a month. MacDonald senior allegedly arranged to pay Hough $11,000 a month from tribal funds, $10,000 of which went to the chairman's son.

MacDonald's new attorney, Val Jolley, asserted that this money was not a kickback but either a legitimately earned salary or a gift. But there was little the lawyer could say to dismiss documents proving that MacDonald had paid his daughter's $33,000 college tuition with a loan from a company that built hazardous waste incinerators. At the time of the trial, the loan was still unpaid, and the prosecution asserted that MacDonald had never intended to pay it at all.

Over the next nine days, 23 businessmen testified against MacDonald and his son, and on October 22, MacDonald was found guilty on 41 counts of soliciting and accepting bribes and kickbacks. He was sentenced to 5 years and 335 days in prison and fined $11,000. Rocky MacDonald was also found guilty, sentenced to 18 months in prison, and fined $2,500. As father and son were escorted to the Window Rock jail, Wanda MacDonald told reporters that the verdict was unfair and that the two men were innocent.

Peter MacDonald's name was removed from the ballot, and on November 23, 1990, Peterson Zah was elected president of the Navajo Nation, a position created in 1989 when the tribal government was restructured. "The first order of business is going to be to restore the tribal government so that it once again enjoys a good reputation, integrity, and accountability," Zah told the *New York Times*. As president of the Navajo Nation, he explained, he would be more directly accountable to the new Navajo Nation Council (formerly the Tribal Council) than the chairman had ever been. The government was now divided into three branches, and the tribal president would act as chief executive officer while the council speaker presided over the legislative body.

Bill Donovan, a reporter for the resurrected *Navajo Times*, noted that Zah's challengers, Leonard Haskie and a write-in candidate named George P. Lee, had garnered an unexpectedly large number of votes. Lee maintained close ties with Peter MacDonald, and Donovan believed that "the hard-core MacDonald supporters were voting for Lee as a faction." Betty Reid, the Navajo reporter who broke the "Big Bo" story, knew without a doubt that MacDonald retained the loyalty of many of his fellow Navajos. After her coverage of the scandal appeared in the Gallup *Independent*, Reid was labeled a traitor and a gossip by Navajos throughout the reservation. The reporter actually took part in a Navajo "protection ceremony" after receiving death threats from anonymous MacDonald supporters.

MacDonald, meanwhile, faced two more trials. In January 1991 the Navajo Tribal Court convicted him of attempting to defraud the tribe in the "Big Bo" Ranch purchase and sentenced him to 450 days in prison. Prosecutor Robert Rothstein noted that "what gives us the most pleasure is that this was in a Navajo court, by a Navajo jury, with a Navajo judge, under Navajo law."

In March 1991, the 62-year-old MacDonald stood before a federal grand jury on charges of bribery and racketeering. The prosecution charged MacDonald, his son, and a business associate named Carlos Pimentel with taking control of a computer software company in Leupp, Arizona. When the company's owner needed a loan, MacDonald allegedly pressured the Tribal Council into providing $2.25 million at low interest rates. MacDonald then demanded that Pimentel be made president and chief executive of the company. Pimentel was to pass controlling interest in the company's stock to MacDonald, keeping the transactions secret until MacDonald's term

Following the funeral of Jimmy Dickson, killed during the July 1989 riot over MacDonald's removal from office, Navajo tribemembers carry the casket to a waiting car. MacDonald was found guilty of participating in a plan to take over tribal headquarters.

of office expired. MacDonald was accused of gaining about $5 million worth of stock through this scheme. He was also charged with accepting $39,000 in bribes from Pimentel.

The jury found both MacDonalds guilty, and in November 1992, MacDonald senior was also found guilty of participating in the takeover of tribal headquarters in July 1989—the undertaking that had culminated in a bloody riot and the death of two of his supporters.

"There are probably only two or three people like Peter MacDonald who come along in a generation," the former chairman's longtime associate Edgar Cahn told *Mother Jones*. "They represent a peculiar investment in the destiny of a people. And the questions you have to ask yourself about them are these: Are they better than anyone else on the scene right now? Are they more a force of good or evil?"

Many observers of Peter MacDonald's downfall have tried to answer this question. His transgressions stand in stark contrast to the many reputable programs he instituted during his chairmanship. Few deny that the Navajo tribe is wealthier than it was in 1963, when MacDonald joined the tribal government. In 1970 the annual budget for the Navajo Nation totaled $18 million. According to the *New York Times*, in 1991 the tribe expected to earn $73 million from its reserves of oil, gas, coal, and timber, and from its investments and land rentals. The tribe's own corporate taxes would bring in another $20 million, and federal appropriations amounted to an added $100 million annually. In 1993, alcoholism and unemployment were still widespread among Navajos, but the average income of a reservation dweller had increased from the 1963 figure of $1,000 to $5,000 a year.

Navajos and non-Indians alike have condemned MacDonald's dictatorial behavior and excessive ambition.

A massive crane lifts coal from the San Juan Mine, an 8,200-acre tract of land in northwestern New Mexico. Strip-mining operations initiated in the 1960s and 1970s continue to ravage the Navajo reservation.

At the same time, Jerry Mander notes that the former chairman was a tough negotiator who "succeeded in wresting back some power from the Bureau of Indian Affairs and renegotiating some . . . outrageous [energy] deals." Mander also claims, however, that MacDonald's advocation of the American dream "probably did more to lead Indians away from traditional paths than any Indian before him." President Peterson Zah has been attempting to reassert those traditions since taking office in 1991. With his encouragement, the tribe's language, culture, and history are being taught in the reservation's schools.

Meanwhile, the darker side of Navajo life—a legacy left for the most part by the BIA and international corporations—lives on. Radioactive pollution continues to poison the Navajo reservation. Ever since 94 million gallons of radioactive water were released at Church Rock, the neighboring Navajos have monitored the damage to their livestock and lands. Lena Willie, a sheepherder, told the *New York Times* that many of her lambs were born without legs, and that many of the adult sheep "just die on us."

In June 1993, the *Boston Globe* reported that a mysterious illness had killed 11 people on the Navajo reservation. Health workers determined that the illness was a virus spread through rodent droppings, but rumors persist that the deaths resulted from a chemical leak from one of the reservation's factories.

The Navajo relocation program is continuing at a slow pace. By 1992, 26 Hopis had moved onto the lands vacated by Navajos in the former joint-use area. Some 300 Navajo families remained on what is now called the Hopi Partition Land, staunchly resisting the government's continued attempts to remove them.

In his autobiography, Peter MacDonald has written that all his ambitions would be satisfied if his attempts to merge traditional Navajo philosophy with capitalism would benefit the tribe in the long run. In 1979 he told the *American Indian Journal*:

> The Navajos have a great ability to adapt, so long as that adaptation is something that they do themselves. We went from a horse to a wagon, a wagon to a pickup truck, we're moving from a hogan to houses with electricity and running water, and we're moving from a sheepherding and an agricultural economy into an industrial and commercial economy. . . . The ability of the Navajos is to adapt to things they feel will benefit their life and will enhance their own physical and personal well-being without sacrificing the independence, sovereignty, the culture, or tradition they have always held on to.

Throughout a dynamic, often troubled career, MacDonald's faith in the Navajo future has survived.

CHRONOLOGY

Spring 1928   Born Hoshkaisith Begay near Teec Nos Pos, Arizona

1944   Drafted into U.S. Marines; stationed in Hawaii and China

1957   Receives Bachelor of Science degree from Oklahoma State University at Norman; begins work at the Hughes Aircraft Corporation as a junior engineer

1963   Returns to Navajo reservation to work for tribal government

1970   Elected chairman of the Navajo Nation; re-elected in 1974 and 1978

1982   Loses election to Peterson Zah

1986   Re-elected chairman for a fourth term

1987   Presides over Navajo economic summit; plays a role in the fraudulent purchase of the Big Boquillas Ranch

1989   Placed on administrative leave; MacDonald's supporters demonstrate on his behalf in front of the Navajo administration and finance building, rioting when tribal police arrive; two protesters are killed

1991   MacDonald begins serving time in Window Rock jail

FURTHER READING

Benedek, Emily. *The Wind Won't Know Me: A History of the Navajo-Hopi Land Dispute.* New York: Alfred A. Knopf, 1992.

Gilbreath, Kent. *Red Capitalism: An Analysis of the Navajo Economy.* Norman: University of Oklahoma Press, 1973.

Iverson, Peter. *The Navajo Nation.* Albuquerque: University of New Mexico Press, 1983.

————. *The Navajos.* New York: Chelsea House Publishers, 1990.

————. "Peter MacDonald." In *American Indian Leaders: Studies in Diversity.* Edited by R. David Edmunds. Lincoln: University of Nebraska Press, 1980.

Kammer, Jerry. *The Second Long Walk.* Albuquerque: University of New Mexico Press, 1980.

MacDonald, Peter, with Ted Schwartz. *The Last Warrior.* New York: Knightsbridge Publishing Co., 1993.

Matthiessen, Peter. *Indian Country.* New York: Viking Press, 1984.

Young, Robert W. *A Political History of the Navajo Tribe.* Tsaile, AZ: Navajo Community College Press, 1978.

INDEX

PICTURE CREDITS

CELIA BLAND has published poetry, reviews, and interviews in a variety of magazines; she is also the author of the Chelsea House biographies *Harriet Beecher Stowe, Osceola*, and *Pontiac*. Bland, who lives in Brooklyn, New York, has taught literature, composition, and creative writing at New York University and Parson's School of Design. Of Cherokee descent, she is particularly interested in writing about Native Americans.

W. DAVID BAIRD is the Howard A. White Professor of History at Pepperdine University in Malibu, California. He holds a Ph.D. from the University of Oklahoma and was formerly on the faculty of history at the University of Arkansas, Fayetteville, and Oklahoma State University. He has served as president of both the Western History Association, a professional organization, and Phi Alpha Theta, the international honor society for students of history. Dr. Baird is also the author of *The Quapaw Indians: A History of the Downstream People* and *Peter Pitchlynn: Chief of the Choctaws* and the editor of *A Creek Warrior of the Confederacy: The Autobiography of Chief G. W. Grayson.*